The Power of

Acceptance

Beyond the Law of Attraction

The Power of Acceptance
by Doreen Banaszak and Arden Rembert Brink

Published by On The Brink Publishing
517 E 1400 N
Centerville, UT 84014

ISBN: 978-0-9832065-2-1 [paperback]
ISBN: 978-0-9832065-3-8 [eBook/PDF]

www.the-power-of-acceptance.com

ALSO BY DOREEN BANASZAK
www.doreenbanaszak.com

Excuse Me, Your Life Is Now

Excuse Me, College Is Now

ALSO BY ARDEN REMBERT BRINK
ardenrembertbrink.com

Unraveling the Mysteries of Moving to Costa Rica

Reality Check, A Real-Life Look at Living in Paradise
~ Release Date: July 2015

The Power of Acceptance

Beyond the Law of Attraction

Become a conscious creator.
Learn how acceptance is the key to
having everything you desire.

Doreen Banaszak
Arden Rembert Brink

WORDS OF PRAISE FOR *THE POWER OF ACCEPTANCE*

Doreen and Arden have created a wonderful and captivating story filled with insights that will change your life! The story draws you right in so much that you wish you were a part of it. Then the practical and easy ways to apply it will truly make a difference in how you can attract and create anything you want into your world.... I highly recommend this book to anyone who is truly interested in the missing link to the Law of Attraction!!
Namaste.
~ *Maureen Saba · global entrepreneur*

Acceptance, the art and the science of living life to your fullest potential, is a key foundational piece to creating more of what you want in life. It is a simple concept and practice and yet at times it is counter-intuitive. I have worked with Doreen for many years and am truly excited to have this concept called out and highlighted through this insightful manuscript. It applies to all aspects of living life, both personally and professionally. It will be a pleasure to recommend or gift this book to many whom I come into contact with that are struggling needlessly.

~ *Karen Powell · friend, colleague, avid supporter, and entrepreneur*

When a colleague told me, "you should be enjoying your success more" something resonated with me. It's been four years since I picked up Doreen's first book and shortly after started a coaching relationship. I just don't know if my words can accurately explain the impact she has had in my life, my business, and general well-being. I am very confident something in this book will connect with you, and your life will be better as well. You'll find yourself and your thoughts throughout its words and pages many times. I know there is no recipe for making life not so hard. But I think you'll find something different in Doreen's approach. You'll find a path to wellbeing that is as real and tangible as the keyboard I'm using to type this.

~Philip J. Statz · husband, father, friend
President, Insight Financial Group, Inc.

FOREWORD

When my friend and coach, Doreen Banaszak, told me about her collaboration with Arden Rembert Brink, I got pretty excited. Combining Arden's excellent storytelling with Doreen's inimitable law of attraction teachings sounded like a sure winner. So I started giving back the motivation Doreen has always freely shared with me as she helped me grow into a best-selling law of attraction author.

I must admit, though, my reason for spurring on Doreen and Arden was self-serving. I wanted to read this book!

Having written six books so far, I've learned that each one has a gestation period. Like a baby, a book isn't born until it has decided that the time is right to finally come on out. The "baby" you now hold took almost two years, but Doreen and Arden are finally the proud parents of *The Power of Acceptance: Beyond the Law of Attraction.*

I dove right into this book, as I'm sure you're looking forward to doing. Arden's skill at building characters and weaving plots is evident from the get-go. As someone who loves a great story, I'm a huge admirer of Arden's talent and craftsmanship. You'll enjoy getting to know and care about the characters in *The Power of Acceptance.*

Doreen doesn't disappoint either, delivering a bounty of practical tools and techniques as we've become accustomed to from her writing. Doreen's ability to teach has made her a sought-after coach; her coaching has been very important for my growth as an author and new thought leader. Lucky for all of us, Doreen writes like she teachers—no filler/all killer.

With Doreen's techniques forming the perfect complement to Arden's story, *The Power of Acceptance* is a wonderful one-two, spiritual "punch." How exciting is it to find a book that takes you on a thrilling emotional journey followed by practical guidance for applying all the principles revealed by that journey? And when you consider that infusing new ideas with emotion virtually super-glues them to your subconscious, I trust the power of this approach will be both appreciated and welcomed.

My favorite thing about *The Power of Acceptance*, however, is not its unique storytelling approach, nor even the two wonderful authors who wrote it. As the title advertises, acceptance is the thread that ties the entire book together. And the focus on acceptance is what makes me treasure this book so much. As with many other things in life, we're often surprised when we learn we've been overlooking something simple and powerful, right underneath our noses.

Who among us hasn't taken acceptance for granted as a tool to help us manifest our desires? Acceptance has, of course, been a foundational component of Doreen's teaching for years and it's a wonderful tool for all of us. But, since you already know all about acceptance, who can blame you for saying, "What's the big deal about it?"

Allow me to explain.

It is imperative for you to stop looking at your current, displeasing material experiences as the "way it is" about which you can do little to change. In fact, your material experiences are not only subjective, they are actually only a reflection of your beliefs. The beliefs you've carried with you into this moment are being reflected back to you constantly in the form of your material reality.

Your displeasing material experiences are, thus, not a reflection of you. Instead they are reflections created by a set of subjective rules you've been given—your beliefs. Knowing this, there is truly no longer any need to beat yourself up, nor blame yourself, for those frustrating and painful aspects of your material reality. And once you start changing your beliefs, rather than trying to change the displeasing "things" themselves, you really can align them with your desires. Doing this puts your focus on your beliefs, the source of those displeasing reflections, and you're continually engaging in the true solution to all your suffering.

And as long as you keep intentionally aligning your beliefs with your desires, the reflections your new beliefs create will grow correspondingly more pleasing.

Improving your beliefs, to align with your desires, is a process anyone can learn to do. It does take practice and a little time. Precisely why Doreen reminds us, time and again, how valuable acceptance is for navigating the gap between your displeasing material experiences in this time/space and the new reflections your newly aligned beliefs will be providing you. Acceptance is, indeed, an often over-looked tool—a powerful and effective technique ready for you to use right now.

I'll definitely be using what I've learned about acceptance in this book. And I'm sure you, too, will find ample value here. If I'm right about that, please share the good news and recommend *The Power of Acceptance* to all your friends. Just as I've done, here, with you!

~ Greg Kuhn
Best-selling author of the Why Quantum Physicists *book series*

www.whyquantumphysicists.com

O be strong then, and brave,
    pure, patient and true;
The work that is yours let no
    other hand do.
For the strength for all need is
    faithfully given
From the fountain within you—
    the kingdom of Heaven.

~ Neville

—Prologue

What if the "power" were really within me? What if the power to be, to do, to have, to know anything were inside of me and all I had to do to awaken it was to simply acknowledge it and allow it to give me all I ever wanted? What if I had the power to love, to be loved all the time, no matter the circumstances, no matter who the person. What if I had the power to not only understand, but to actually KNOW and had the courage to live MY truth. What if I actually consciously used this power to create my life? What if?

What if my cycles of fear, self-doubt, confusion and self-loathing just stopped? What if all of a sudden I was worthy, I was deserving, I was valuable? What if I were no longer separated from the things I really, truly, wanted? What if for me there was no more longing, frustration, lack? What if I were fulfilled, overflowing with any and all experiences I chose? What if?

What if it really was always right inside of me, this power to be, to do, to have, to know anything? What if they were right, the prophets, the philosophers, the theologians, the artists, and the scientists? What if "the kingdom was within," "heaven was on earth," and I did "have all that I could ever want right in the palm of my hand?" What if it was all true and I went through life not living this truth? What if?

What if God, the Universe, Source, only wanted for me to be happy, just be happy and everything I ever wanted would spring from that happiness? What if I really was a god all along and I lived my life in denial of what I really am? What if there was never any reason to suffer? What if this power was never locked away, was never out of my reach, and was never in need of me seeking or finding it? What if?

What if I was willing to consider that all the "what ifs" might be true? That the power is within me, right now? That I could create a life I love? What if I changed, "What if" to "Why not?"

How would my life change if I was willing to consider why not? Would I experience more joy, wealth, love, and abundance? It would make sense that I would experience a lot more, but how? I want to believe why not for me, but I have lived my life not believing in these "what ifs." How do I start now?

~ Doreen Banaszak

Part One

Arden Rembert Brink

—Chapter 1

Allison pulled her minivan into the driveway, sighing to herself as the peeling paint on the garage came into view. *Really*, she thought for the hundredth time, *we've got to get that painted.*

That thought, though, was immediately followed —as it always seemed to be—by a little clutch of fear in the pit of her stomach. They couldn't afford to paint the garage. Not unless she got that bonus at work, and even then it seemed like the five thousand dollars that she was hoping for had been mentally spent about five times over.

The little clutch of fear got a little bit bigger. What if the bonus turned out to be less than she was expecting? Worse, still, what if she didn't get one at all?

Allison knew her work had been good the past year, but business was down overall and that coupled with the Henderson project that hadn't actually gone so well... it wasn't unimaginable that the company would hand out only token bonuses, if any at all.

She parked the car and gathered up her briefcase, lunch bag, and umbrella.

At least, she thought, trying to look on the bright

side, the rain had finally stopped and it looked like it would be a nice evening. And her heirloom tomatoes would be grateful for the good ground-soaking they'd finally gotten. First time she'd tried growing tomatoes and this year's drought wasn't helping.

Rick met her at the door with a kiss and relieved her of the heavy briefcase, carrying it into the living room for her. He knew she'd be back at work on her laptop after dinner, so there was no point in putting the briefcase very far away.

"I got home a little early so I got started on some spaghetti sauce," Rick reported as he poured Allison a glass of wine. "But if you're okay to take over now, I really need to go make a few calls. I think there's someone else bidding for that McMillan house and I need to see if I can find out anything about who it is."

"Sure, of course." She kicked off her high heels, rolled up her sleeves, and started pulling crisp lettuce, scallions, and cucumbers out of the refrigerator. A few minutes later she had a salad laid out on plates and went back to the stove to stir the spaghetti sauce.

Allison took a small sip of wine and gently stirred the sauce. Her thoughts slowly returned to where they'd been before being derailed by the peeling garage paint.

That book she'd picked up at the bookstore a couple of weeks ago seemed to be on her mind a lot lately. Acceptance, it kept talking about. Acceptance and being "willing to consider."

Accepting your state of being seemed to be a key. The only problem was that she wasn't so sure it was a key she could accept.

"Ha!" she said accusingly to herself. "Did you just hear yourself? You can't *accept* the idea of *acceptance*? How are you ever going to get anywhere with this manifesting stuff if you can't even a grip on one of the basic ideas?"

That had begun to nag at her as a possible ongoing problem—it seemed that now that she better understood the concepts of the Law of Attraction and conscious creation, the more she was afraid that her fear was going to make things even worse. If you attract what you think about, was she going to attract not getting her bonus because that's what she seemed to think about a lot lately?

But as she hypnotically stirred the bubbling red sauce, an answering little voice from inside came back at her. "The book says I could just accept my state of being. So what's my state of being right now?"

The wooden spoon paused mid-stir. "My state of being is *annoyed*. Annoyed and..." she stopped, frozen in place. "What else? Well yeah, *fearful*. I'm afraid I won't ever really 'get it' and I feel like I'm going to jinx this bonus with my fear and negative thinking."

"I don't want to be afraid and I sure don't want to go down some weird bad-attitude rabbit hole and cause my bonus to go away. Sheesh."

Oddly enough though, the more she stirred, the more the thought came to her, "What if I really *could* just accept that my state of being is one of annoyance and fear.

"What if I really *could* just allow the possibility that even though I'm really kinda scared in this moment, maybe it's okay. Maybe accepting would be better than trying to resist."

At first it seemed a little crazy. This is exactly what she'd been wrestling with ever since she first started reading this book.

Shouldn't she be *resisting* thoughts that she didn't want? She didn't want to be scared about not getting the bonus she needed and she didn't want to have to look at the peeling paint on the garage and worry about water damage to the wood underneath.

Didn't accepting it mean that she was saying that those things were okay?

"They're not okay!" she found herself muttering aloud as she dragged the big pot out of the cabinet to cook the pasta. "I don't want those things in my life!"

Maybe then she could just accept that she was experiencing resistance—a lot of resistance—to the idea of accepting circumstances that she didn't want.

"Maybe I could be willing," she thought, "to just *consider* that I might let go of that resistance at some point in the future."

"I could do that," she said after a long moment's pause. "I'm not actually saying it's okay right now, I'm just allowing that it might be okay in the future. Yeah…. I could live with that."

As she let that thought wash softly over her, she found that the knot in her stomach seemed to be gone. Her first thought was that her glass of wine must have been kicking in, until she glanced over and realized that it was still sitting there, full other than the very first small sip she'd taken twenty minutes ago.

"Hmmm…." the idea surfaced, "maybe accepting what I'm experiencing as a state of being *really* is better than resisting it."

Rick bounced back into the kitchen, with a puzzled smile on his face. "You'll never guess what just happened."

"Okay, you're right." Allison grinned back at him. "So maybe you can just tell me."

He shook his head. "What a weird thing. So… first I called Paul McMillan to ask if he was really getting someone else to bid. I thought he was really happy with the last project we did for him, so I just wanted to hear it straight from him.

"Turns out that that new company, Taylor

Construction—remember I was telling you about them? —anyway, they approached Paul and really pushed him to let them bid the job, but he told them no, that he had always been more than satisfied with my price and quality and that I had the contract. Gotta tell you, I'm relieved about that. I've been counting on that job."

"That's great," Allison said as she served up the spaghetti. "Really, I'm so relieved, too."

"But wait," Rick replied. "That's not the weird part.

"Right after that, Mike called and made us the greatest offer. He'd been paid a flat rate for that painting job over on 3rd Avenue, including the paint. Remember he was telling us about those folks who liked our paint color, so he'd used the same color for their house. They were running this promotion on five-gallon buckets at the paint store for custom paint, so he ended up buying a lot more paint than he needed for less money than he would've spent just buying the regular gallons he needed for that job.

"Any-hoo, he got the job done more quickly than he'd planned, and he's already been paid for the week and he has this extra paint that matches ours. How random is that?!?

"He offered to come this week and paint our garage and have us pay him later when he's doing the painting on the McMillan job. He figures he'll need the money more then. So we agreed I would just add two bucks extra to his hourly pay then until the total cost of painting the garage is paid off, and he'll give us the paint for free."

"What a bizarre coincidence." He shook his head again. "Dinner looks great."

Allison shook her head a little bit, too. Coincidence? *Really*??

Maybe there was something to this accepting thing after all.

Allison plumped up the pillows and settled in to bed with her book. She found herself staring at the pages, drifting in her mind back two weeks.

Her workday had been even more frustrating than most. She loved working with her clients and knew she was good at it but Randall, her boss, had chewed her out that day for not trying to up-sell the Wolforths on several features in their home. He was insisting that they could have had a higher profit margin if she had.

She had tried to explain that just because they were approved for a larger mortgage didn't actually mean they could *afford* a more expensive house. She had developed a strong rapport with Marshall and Sandra Wolforth during the design process and they'd confided in her about some challenges in their finances that they hadn't told the bank about.

She'd had to convince her boss that *because* she hadn't tried to push them into features they couldn't afford, they'd *stayed* with their company, they were *very* happy clients, and already she had a *referral* from them for another home to build for a friend.

That last bit about the referral had shut her boss up slightly, but she was still miffed that she'd had to argue with him at all. She knew she was great with the clients and good for business, why couldn't *he* see that.

She'd had the argument with Randall just before noon, leaving her stomach still churning when her lunch hour came at 12:30, so instead of eating right away she drove over to Center Street and pulled into the first empty parking spot she saw.

Even though she liked the ease of shopping out at the big-box stores on the highway as much as the next person, she really loved the old-fashioned feel of Center Street, with its eclectic variety of small shops, and wandering down the street window-shopping helped soothe her.

When she saw Lagniappe, the little bookstore, the thought occurred to her that there was probably a book that could help. Maybe something about dealing with difficult bosses, or how to be more valued at work, or maybe just how to deal with your mid-life crisis.

It seemed so trite, but that's what she felt like she was having—a crisis, although maybe not of life and death proportions. In fact, she felt a little silly as the word "crisis" formed in her mind. *It wasn't that bad*, she thought to herself.

But, hell, some days—like today—it felt that bad.

As Allison approached the main counter, the woman standing there looked up at her with a broad smile. It was a smile that just made you want to smile back, which Allison found herself doing, despite her dour mood.

It was a kind smile, the sort that seemed to say, "Whatever is going on in your life right now, it will be a little bit better now that you're here."

"I'm looking for your 'self-help' section," Allison said softly, realizing as she said it that it felt a little like an admission of guilt. "Maybe something on asserting yourself or increasing your self-confidence or something like that?"

The woman came out from behind the counter and stretched her smooth, tanned, and slightly plump hand out to Allison. "Marjorie Parker. Welcome to Lagniappe."

"My name's Allison." She noticed Marjorie pronounced it "lan-yap" with that slightly nasally French sound where the "g" and "n" came together. "Where does the name 'Lagniappe' come from?"

"It's a French Cajun term. Means 'a little something extra' which I've always thought was a great way to approach life. Give it a little something extra!" Marjorie waved her arm around at their cozy surroundings. "It's what I try to do with the shop. Give a little something extra."

She led Allison through the racks of books, past the overstuffed armchairs, to a section back near the café. "Here's my 'Personal Development' section."

She wrinkled up her nose and shook her head slightly. "I don't like the name 'self-help' actually—it always sounds to me like someone who thinks they're broken and need fixing. Truly, I believe that we're all just perfect, just the way we are.

"Of course, I *do* realize that sometimes we need some encouragement to get out of our own way and allow that perfection to shine through!" She smiled again at Allison. "I have some books that can help with that!"

"Would you like to sit down and have a cup of tea? Maybe if you told me a little bit more about what you feel like you need, I could help point you to the right book."

Marjorie led them over to one of the few empty tables in the small café and motioned to Allison to sit down. "Cup of tea or cold drink? Or would you like something more? Are you on your lunch break?"

Allison realized that the combination of her stroll down Center Street and Marjorie's friendly demeanor had eased the churning in her stomach. She looked at the menu card on the table with interest. "Wow, this bacon, brie, and sprout sandwich on a croissant sounds great! I'd love one of those." She added, "and an iced tea, please."

Marjorie went up to the counter to put in the order and came back with two glasses. "Our secret recipe iced tea—see how you like it."

Allison took a small taste followed by a large gulp. "This is great. Can you tell me what's in it?"

"Well then, it wouldn't be a secret recipe any more, would it?" Marjorie smiled. "Tell me what's sent you looking for 'self-help' books."

Despite having known Marjorie for all of three minutes, Allison found herself pouring out her situation to her. She described the entire argument with Randall at the office that morning and found herself sputtering again with frustration.

"I wouldn't mind if he just asked me about their situation. But he started right off bitching at me, assuming I'd made a *mistake* rather than assuming I'd made a *good decision* that he might just not yet understand. That's a huge difference!" She slammed her glass down on the table.

"Sorry," she muttered sheepishly to Marjorie as the secret-recipe tea splashed over the table. "But I just feel so frustrated. I'm good at my job. I know I am.

"But here I am, I'm forty-four years old, I've worked at this company for over ten years and in the field virtually my entire career, and I'm still struggling to make enough money to be able to paint my freaking garage!

"I just can't figure out if there's something wrong with this particular job, or with how I'm handling it, or with me.

"But the idea of starting over in some whole new career scares me to death and, besides, I'm *good* at this job."

Marjorie looked at her sympathetically. "Not," Allison said wryly, "that you'd know it to talk to my boss. What the hell is wrong with him?"

Their lunch arrived just then and conversation halted while they bit into their sandwiches.

Allison rolled her eyes back and chewed appreciatively. "This is *really* good."

Marjorie sensed that Allison's tirade had petered out, or at least was taking a break while she ate. "You know," she said gently. "I do know of a book that might really help you. It's something that I found some years ago and has really made a difference in *my* life."

She took a bite of her own sandwich, an avocado, grilled red pepper, and feta roll-up, and continued. "You read a lot these days about how our thoughts turn into things, how we need to think positively, and we create our own reality. Some folks call it the Law of Attraction —although I think that can be sometimes be confusing.

"I believe all of that, but I think that there's something often missing in how people approach that. It's as though they try to *force* themselves to think positively, to *make* good things manifest, when it's really all about *allowing* the good that already exists to come to them."

Marjorie saw that Allison was listening intently, so she continued. "It's easy to *say* 'just allow it' but most people don't have a clue how to do that. I know I didn't.

"The starting point is to *accept* your state of being. Even when that state of being is resistance or frustration or something else that we think of as negative. That's one of the things I learned from this book."

At that, Allison's unconscious nodding "yes" that Marjorie had noticed turned to a subtle shaking her head in disagreement. "But I don't want to accept my frustration!" she exclaimed impatiently. "I don't want to be in the situation that's causing my frustration! Why would I want to accept *that*?!?"

The gentle shaking her head "no" had now turned to vigorous indication that she did not agree with Marjorie at all. Marjorie sat back and sipped her tea. She'd seen this reaction before.

"You've heard the expression 'what we resist persists' haven't you? That's all this is really about— letting go of the resistance so that you can be more open so that there's 'room' inside you to allow in something better than the thing you're resisting." She knew from experience it was best to leave it at that.

Allison was still shaking her head. "I just don't see how 'accepting'," as she made quotation marks in the air with her hands, "the resistance will result in letting go of it." She swallowed the last bite of her sandwich and tucked her napkin under her plate. "I want to get rid of what I don't want, not accept it.

"I need to get back to work anyway. Where do I pay for lunch?" Allison realized that she might have sounded a bit harsh to Marjorie and didn't want to leave on a sour note. "That really was a yummy sandwich."

"My treat," Marjorie replied. "I enjoyed talking with you, and now that you know the food here is good, hopefully you'll come back more often." She smiled genuinely at Allison, relieving her of any worries that she'd been rude by disagreeing so violently. "And if you find that you re-think that book, there are several copies on the shelf. As I say, it's one of my favorites so I try to keep a good supply on hand."

The next day at work Allison found herself thinking back to Marjorie, Lagniappe, her sandwich, and the book. She still didn't think the book sounded like what she was after, but when her lunchtime rolled around she found herself driving over to Center Street, almost without even making a conscious decision to do so. As she parked, she told herself it was only for another of those great sandwiches.

Marjorie was busy with another customer when Allison arrived, so she headed back to the café and ordered a sandwich to go. *Might as well check out that Personal Growth section of books while I'm waiting on my order*, she thought, as she wandered over to the shelves.

She glanced at a few titles, but nothing jumped out at her until she came to three copies of *The Power of Acceptance.* She plucked one copy off the shelf and looked at the blurb on the back cover.

"Acceptance is your natural state," it declared, "and acceptance opens you up to allowing in all the good that is yours. It's all there, ready for you, but as long as you're resisting, there's no room for it to come to you."

She opened the book and flipped through the pages, pausing when a passage caught her eye. "Trying to change your circumstances without being aware of your state of being is only expanding more opportunities to experience more of your state of being. And if you don't like your current state of being, why would you want to experience more of that?"

And a few pages later, "I realized that I had spent a lot of time running away from, or resisting certain states of being—hate, fear, failure. I had also spent a lot of time chasing other states of being like happiness, wealth, abundance, and joy.

"Well, if I'm resisting in one direction and trying to chase in another, the only place I could end up is stuck between the two. And remember, these states of being exist inside of us right now, so you can't out run them and there is no reason to chase them, they are already there.

"If resisting states of being I didn't want to experience expanded my experience with them, then it was time again to consider the opposite—What if I *accepted* my state of being instead of resisting it?."

Although Allison still didn't feel like she agreed with everything the book was saying, or even totally understood it, somehow reading it felt good. It felt like it was opening up a possibility of looking at something a different way, and while she couldn't explain it, even to herself, she liked the way that felt.

They called her name at the café window and she picked up her sandwich, taking it and the book to the front counter to pay. Marjorie greeted her warmly and sincerely as Allison handed her the book and the café bill.

"I thought maybe I'd give the book a try after all,"

she explained to Marjorie with a slightly self-conscious shrug. "And I had to have another of those sandwiches!"

Marjorie rang up her purchases and dropped a small additional item into the bag. "Have a praline, on the house." She handed the bag to Allison. "It's a New Orleans candy that isn't very well-known around here, but they're one of my favorites and we made a big batch this morning. Thought folks might enjoy trying something different.

"In general I tend to stay away from sugar, but I think a treat now and then keeps you from feeling deprived. Hope you enjoy it."

"And the book," she added as Allison thanked her and headed for the door.

Allison's sleepy eyes re-focused on the page in front of her. She looked over to see Rick staring at her. "What?" she asked.

"You haven't turned a page in fifteen minutes," he said, puzzling over her behavior. "Doing some deep thinking?"

"Just doing a little time-traveling, remembering when I met Marjorie at Lagniappe a couple of weeks ago and got this book."

Allison realized that as she'd drifted back in time for those moments, she'd also used up her brief before-bed reading time, so she put the bookmark in place, set the book on her nightstand, and turned out the light. Lots to think about, but she was too tired at the moment. She'd let it just percolate while she slept. She leaned over to kiss Rick goodnight and was asleep almost before her head was back on her own pillow.

––––––––––––––––––––

Allison woke up the next morning energized and happy. Her morning at work went smoothly and it seemed that lunchtime was there before she knew it. She wasn't surprised to find that she wanted to head over to Lagniappe. She hoped Marjorie wouldn't be too busy to talk.

Her heart sank when a quick scan of the bookshop didn't show Marjorie anywhere. The man working the front counter, though, reassured her that Marjorie had just stepped back into the stockroom and pointed the way for Allison.

She slipped behind the shoji screen that shielded the open doorway and stuck her head into the stock room. "Got a minute?" she asked Marjorie tentatively.

"Of course," was Marjorie's quick reply. "I was ready for a break anyway—I was just reviewing some old stock that I think I'll put on a clearance sale. Why don't we go out to the café? If you're interested, we just put a new salad on the menu—it's mixed baby greens, blue cheese, and sliced strawberries, topped with a crab cake."

After they ordered and settled in to their seats, Allison told Marjorie about her experience the night before—struggling with the idea of accepting her state of being, even though she didn't want that state of being to continue, and how much better she felt after she finally tried it.

"It still doesn't seem to make sense to me, but I have to say it feels like it worked, so something must be right." She looked puzzled. "I still don't think I fully get it, though, the idea that you need to accept your current state of being, even when that's the thing you want to change."

"Really, I do understand what you mean," said Marjorie, nodding. "I had the same struggle at first. But, here's how I gradually came to understand it—our natural state is actually abundance...abundance in our health, our relationships, our work, our finances. But we have a tendency to get in our own way and prevent that natural abundance from flowing to us. The resistance that we feel when things seem to be going wrong is actually our deep inner being knowing that we're standing in our own way.

"The more we resist, the more we seem to have opportunities to experience resistance. In other words, the more 'bad stuff' seems to happen to us, giving us more things to resist.

"So by noticing our state of being—that we're

resisting what's going on around us, the stuff we don't like and don't want—we have the choice to accept that, and by choosing acceptance, we gradually create more opportunities to experience things we want to accept, that is, the 'good things.'

"I know it can seem counter-intuitive at first, but accepting that you're experiencing resistance, then you're actually no longer *in* a state of *resistance*, you're in a state of *acceptance*, so you're changing the cause. Once you change the cause, then the effect will change."

Allison nodded and finished chewing a bit of crab cake and salad so that she could speak. "Keep this on the menu, it's great! I think I know what you mean about changing the cause.

"This morning during my coffee break I grabbed the book to read a few pages, and it was talking about the idea that most of the time we focus on the outcome, which it called the reflection of our state of being, that is, the physical reality, when what we really need to be focusing on is the cause, or the state of being.

"The book gave the analogy of trying to fix a mistake on a document you printed off the computer by erasing the mistake on the paper rather than going back into your file on the computer and making the change there. It might be fixed temporarily on that one page, but the next time you print it, it will still be there. Trying to fix the outcome can never be more than temporary. You've got to fix the source, it said."

"Yes," Marjorie agreed. "And fixing the source happens by accepting your state of being. Which you did last night, and good things happened. Mostly you felt better, and that's the key. Feeling good like that indicates that you're experiencing your true natural state, which is abundance."

"Well," Allison added, "then Rick came out and told me about these almost magical solutions to a couple of problems. I mean, is it possible that those good results came from my accepting my state of being that I had just been doing? That has to just be a crazy coincidence, isn't it?"

"Could I make a suggestion?" Marjorie asked. "What if you didn't try to analyze and figure out whether it was the result of your accepting or not. What if you actually just accepted those things as well? Appreciated them, even, without trying to analyze them.

"So often, when people start trying to understand the ideas of conscious creation, law of attraction and so on, they decide on some big thing they want. Then they spend all their time judging whether that thing is manifesting for them or not. They forget to notice and appreciate the small things that happen along the way.

"All that analyzing and judging and evaluating is just more resistance, so their 'state of being' is one of resistance rather than acceptance.

"I've found it works really well for me to notice all the small gifts in the course of a day—whether something as simple as a pleasant smile from someone that made me feel good or something much larger like this opportunity to get your garage painted. Just appreciate them and don't try to analyze them.

"The idea is that the more you appreciate, that's what expands, so the more things show up to appreciate. You're *allowing* your natural good in."

Allison was thoughtful as she took her last bite. "I hear you. It's just hard for me not to analyze things —I feel like I need to understand why and how something works. It's just who I am."

"So..." Marjorie smiled gently at her. "If you did fully understand why and how it works, what would that mean? What would your state of being be?"

"Well," she paused. "I'd feel comfortable, I'd feel in-control, I'd feel more powerful because I really *got it.*"

Marjorie pressed on, "Could you *consider* that it would be *possible* to feel comfortable, in-control, and more powerful even if you didn't fully understand how and why it works?" She smiled reassuringly. "You don't have to actually *feel* comfortable, in-control, and so on right in this moment. That's likely to be too big a leap, I understand. Just might you be willing to *consider* that it could be *possible*?"

She pulled out a piece of paper from her pocket

and looked at it. "A grocery list I found in one of those books I was just working with. I'll bet someone got to the grocery store and wondered what in the world they'd done with their list!" She turned it over and wrote out a couple of lines in her neat handwriting, then handed the paper to Allison.

"I accept that I'm experiencing resistance right now and that's okay. I'm willing to consider the possibility that I don't need to understand in order to experience comfort, control, and power right now." Allison read the two sentences out loud and looked questioningly at Marjorie.

"You'll read lots more about this the further you get into the book, but it might be worth just playing around a little with actually saying those to yourself. See what, if anything, happens for you."

The sun was getting low in the sky when Marjorie pulled into her driveway. She waved at her next-door neighbor as she reached into the back of her Subaru Outback for her grocery bags. *He's a good-looking fellow,* she thought to herself, *but he sure seems adrift. He never seems to look very happy.*

She knew the young man was the son-in-law of Walt and Louise, her neighbors, and that he and his wife, Roxanne, had moved a few months ago into the little basement apartment at Roxanne's parents' house.

Her downstairs neighbor reported that she'd heard the young man had lost his job a couple of years ago and hadn't been able to get another one, and that the bank had foreclosed on the house that he and Rox owned. That's why they were living with Walt and Louise now.

She didn't know if that was true, but it did seem to fit his demeanor and appearance. He always waved and was pleasant enough, but Marjorie thought he looked a bit like someone who'd had the stuffing knocked out of him.

She shook her head slightly as she went inside, wondering what had actually happened to this nice young man. Or, more to the point, what was ahead for him.

—Chapter 2

Dianne Sanchez was annoyed that her regular coffee shop was temporarily closed. She understood— with the street and sidewalk all torn up out front there was no easy or even safe access—but she was still annoyed. It threw her whole morning routine off, and Dianne liked her routines.

Driving down Center Street last week, she'd noticed a bookshop called Lagniappe that had a café and the sign in the window had proclaimed "Open early for your morning coffee!" *I suppose I could give that place a try,* she thought, grudgingly.

Center Street was still quiet at this hour—most of the shops didn't open until later—and she pulled her Lexus into a spot right in front of the door and parked. Despite feeling grumpy about the disruption of her morning routine, she couldn't help but smile as she entered the shop. It just had a *feeling* about it that seemed to soothe her spirit right away.

Dianne glanced around the bookstore, looking for the café so should she could grab her latte and run, and noticed an attractive woman carrying flowers through the store toward the back. Guessing she was taking them for the café tables, Dianne followed her, thinking as she went that the tall woman with the sandy blonde hair seemed familiar somehow. *Is that Marjorie Parker?* she wondered to herself. *But Marjorie is much heavier than that.*

In fact, the Marjorie Parker she remembered from years ago at Maxwell Pharmaceuticals had been downright fat, she thought unkindly. This woman was ever so slightly plumpish, but it seemed to suit her somehow. She certainly wasn't fat.

With Dianne's long, all-business stride and the other woman taking her time carrying her box full of little flower vases, they arrived at the café in the back of the bookshop at the same time. The woman set her box down and turned to Dianne with a welcoming smile.

"What could I get for you this morning?" she asked, followed almost immediately by a tentative, "Dianne?"

"It *is* you," Dianne replied. "I *thought* so but wasn't sure. I guess I haven't seen you since you left Maxwell... how many years has that been now?" Before she could filter out the potentially rude remark, she blurted out, "You've lost so much weight!"

"It's been almost fifteen years." Marjorie smiled again, clearly not offended. "And a bit more than fifty pounds."

"Wow," Dianne was shaking her head in

amazement. "Well, you look great. Not just the weight but you look so relaxed and happy. Do you work here?"

Marjorie laughed. "Boy do I ever." She stepped behind the counter and logged into the computer at the cash register. "I own the place. Have for, well, almost fifteen years. This is what I did when I left Maxwell— bought this shop and have been here ever since."

She took in Dianne's sharp business suit, high heels, and chic hairstyle. "You look like you're on your way to the office. Could I get you a coffee or tea or something? We also have a couple of great breakfast sandwiches."

"Can I just get a latte, please? With skim milk." Dianne glanced at her watch and her face tightened slightly. "I'm running late."

"Coming right up," Marjorie replied. "You know, whole milk is actually better for you." She looked up from preparing the latte into Dianne's incredulous face. "Really, it is." She handed over the cup, "you need the fat in the milk to absorb the vitamins."

"Whatever," Dianne muttered as she paid for her latte. "I've gotta run, but it was great to see you. How do you get that nice tan when you're here in the shop all day?"

"I'll walk out with you," Marjorie came out from behind the counter.

"It's true that I'm here in the shop most days, but

I also do a good bit of traveling. I just got back from Costa Rica where I go usually at least once a year. There's a wildlife rehab place I try to support a little and another organization I take books down to for their annual book sale. I just love the mountains there. It's a beautiful country.

"And, as far as tan goes, I try to get out in the sun briefly even when I'm just here—we need our vitamin D, you know. I'm careful not to get too much sun, but I think we did ourselves a disservice when we all got so scared of being out in it at all. Like so many things, what we've been told is bad for us isn't quite as simple as they make it sound."

At that, the two women reached the front door. Dianne extended her hand for a business-like shake goodbye, while Marjorie reached for her with a light hug and kiss on the cheek.

She laughed as Dianne pulled back slightly. "Oh, I always have a hard time with that when I'm first back from Costa Rica. Down there everyone kisses everyone, sort-of like Europe but only one cheek. But I do mean *everyone*—you kiss your housekeeper, you kiss your lawyer, not to mention any stranger you meet. Takes me a while to switch gears once I get back!"

Dianne smiled back. "Well, it was nice to see you again. My regular coffee shop is closed for a couple of days. Maybe I'll stop in again."

It was a busy morning at Maxwell, and Dianne was grateful when her assistant stuck her head in the door with a reminder, "Time for your lunch meeting in the conference room upstairs."

It was an informal meeting with a catered lunch and Dianne was only there to listen to the announcement about the new packaging design. She had no responsibilities for the presentation and she'd already had a sneak preview of the packaging itself, so she didn't really have to pay too much attention. It should be a relaxing hour away from her desk.

Although in past years it was hard to *pry* Dianne away from her desk, she found that more and more she appreciated a little break. She sometimes wondered if maybe the twenty-five years at the job was beginning to catch up with her.

A buffet was being spread on the sideboard in the conference room and Dianne gave it a quick glance before taking her seat. Looked fine, although ordinary enough. The company insisted on using Smithson's Restaurant for their corporate catering, and while their food was adequate, it was certainly uninspired.

The formal unveiling of the new packaging concept was flashy, but quick, and soon Dianne found herself in the buffet line, serving a plate of some kind of goopy chicken dish and an anemic-looking salad that consisted mostly of iceberg lettuce.

Rather than sit back down at the massive table, she stood off to the side of the room and picked at her lunch while she watched her colleagues mingle and talk. The new packaging was very clean and streamlined and she could tell there was a buzz of approval.

Lost in thought, she jumped slightly when a voice near-by asked, "Would you like me to take your plate, or get you anything else?"

She snapped back to the large, glass-walled conference room and looked at the dark-haired waiter standing near here. "Jay" his nametag read and she noticed he was a handsome fellow. Smithson's leaned, she'd always thought, toward dumpy and unattractive wait-staff, so she was a little surprised by the good looks and clearly intelligent face in front of her. He didn't seem like typical Smithson's material.

Dianne looked down at her unfinished lunch and felt self-conscious that she hadn't eaten her food. Growing up as she had, where food on your plate was *never* wasted, she'd never really shaken the feeling that leaving food uneaten was not just wasteful, but a sin of some sort, a lack of respect for the sacrifices and hard work that had put it there.

"Sorry, I didn't finish. I...guess I wasn't as hungry as I thought," she stammered, all the while thinking she was silly to be apologizing to the waiter.

He smiled wryly. "No problem. I wouldn't have finished it either. Actually, I wouldn't have started it."

Dianne looked startled. "Don't you like your restaurant's food?" she asked, surprised at his frankness.

"Well, it's sure not what I'd be cooking if I had any say in the matter," he replied candidly. "Half of it doesn't even qualify as *real food* by my standards. You should see the list of ingredients on some of this stuff."

Dianne now looked puzzled rather than startled. "You mean the list of ingredients in the recipes?"

"Nah," he replied. "What recipes? This stuff all comes pre-made and packaged. I don't even think it's made in a kitchen. A factory is more like it." He shrugged his shoulders slightly. "As I say, not much real food in *this* food."

He stepped a few feet away to pick up some discarded dishes and return them to the service area. After refilling several water glasses at the table, he wandered back over toward Dianne. She smiled to see him coming, somewhat appalled at him critiquing his employer's offerings so freely yet intrigued by his apparently genuine beliefs about food.

"So..." she looked up at him as he reached earshot. "What food would *you* be cooking if you *did* have a say in the matter."

"Well, it would depend on the budget and what

kind of meal the client wanted, of course, but I can promise you there would be a lot more actual *food* in the food.

"You know, when you use freshly grown produce and herbs, organic butter and cream from grass-fed cows, good quality extra virgin olive oil, fruits and vegetables that were picked ripe rather trucked from across the country or worse yet, brought halfway around the world ...when your food is real, ideally locally produced, and properly prepared, you don't need to add all those chemicals, sweeteners, weird additives and so on. It just tastes *good*, all by itself."

Dianne was intrigued. "Do you cook, yourself?" she asked. "That is, could you cater a dinner party? Not Smithson's, but *you*?"

He nodded, "Yeah, actually I do cook, but I don't have a food license or anything. I'd have to do all the actual food preparation at your house. Technically I'd be your 'personal chef' for the party, not a caterer." He cocked his head slightly, searching her face to see if she was just teasing him. "What did you have in mind?"

"I'm giving a dinner party for ten people next month and I think they might be interested in what you're saying about food. I'd like you to consider cooking the dinner, and when you serve it you could tell them a little bit about what the dish was, why it was 'real food' as you're calling it, what makes it special...."

Dianne was a little surprised to hear all of this coming out of her mouth. The idea had never occurred to her until she found herself describing it to Jay, and she wondered briefly if she'd lost her mind. "I think it would be a little bit different than the usual dinner party. It could be fun."

He swallowed hard before saying, "Yes, I could do that. I would really like to do that." This was exactly the kind of thing he'd been thinking about lately, how he wanted to try to earn a living. He'd been out of work for so long now—he didn't count being a server for Smithson's as work, more like some kind of hellish punishment for some unknown crime—that he'd begun to give up on getting a job back in his field.

But, the longer he was out of work and the more time he'd had to read up on the industrialization of our food supply, the more he'd gotten interested in re-creating himself as a personal chef, or something like that, working to help people understand how they really could change how they ate without becoming radicals, food extremists, or never eating hamburgers or pie again.

As his job hunt had become less and less productive and more and more frustrating over the past two years, he'd had more time on his hands and spent some of it watching the great chefs on the television food channels. He'd been learning to cook good food from scratch and found it was easier than he thought, tastier than he'd expected, and more fun that he'd imagined. Now he just needed to figure out a way to turn that growing passion into a viable business.

Maybe catering this dinner could give a jump-start to this new career.

He scribbled down the particulars that Dianne gave him with her contact information and date of the party and went back to work. For once, the rest of the event passed without him sullenly dwelling on how much he hated this job. His body performed the tasks of serving and cleaning up, while his mind was racing with the possibilities of this dinner party... and beyond.

When Jason got home that afternoon he pulled his fifteen-year old Nissan pick-up into the driveway, pulling off to the side so his in-laws could get their car in later. He waved to his neighbor as she came out of her house with her dog. He didn't know what kind of job she had, but she seemed to have flexible hours. He'd seen her leave the house early that morning and now, at only three in the afternoon, she seemed to be home from work. But other times he'd seen her arrive home much later.

In any case, whatever her job was, she must like it. She always seemed happy to him, not that fake bubbly kind of crazy-cheerful like his mother-in-law was—*she* annoyed the hell out of him—but just relaxed and at ease.

He headed downstairs, glad to see that he'd caught Roxanne before she went to work. "Hey hon, glad you're still here. I had the coolest thing happen today."

"Excellent. I want to hear about it, so talk fast. I need to leave soon." Rox pulled her curly hair back off her face into a ponytail. "What happened? I thought you had a catering gig today." She looked at him more closely, noting that he was clearly wearing the required black pants, white shirt, and his nametag. "In fact, I'd say you definitely had a job today. So, what happened?"

"We had some kind of lunch thing over at that drug company today, what's their name, Maxwell? Anyway, I got to talking with some woman there and she ended up offering me a *real* catering gig—one where I'm doing the cooking, not just schlepping crap food around." As he talked, he yanked his nametag from his shirt and laid it on the dresser along with Dianne's business card.

Roxanne looked down at the nametag proclaiming her husband's name to be Jay. "I don't think I understand why you want to do that when you hate being a waiter so much. Look at this, you don't even use your real name you're so embarrassed. No one's called you Jay since high school. Wouldn't you still be having to serve them the food you'd cooked?"

"I don't mind being a waiter," he snapped back. "There's nothing wrong with being a waiter. It's the 'schlepping crap food' around part that I hate. There's just no *food* in Smithson's food. I was putting all that stuff away in the walk-in the other day, the stuff I just served at this lunch meeting. You wouldn't believe the ingredients list on some of those things. Blech." He made a face, leaving no uncertainty about how he felt about Smithson's food. I mean, shouldn't a restaurant actually *make* the food they serve?

"I know I can do this—you've eaten some of the things I've learned to cook. They're good. Really good. I think I found my natural talent." He smiled charmingly. "And get this, the *outstanding* part is that she wants me to not just serve the food, but tell the guests about what they're eating, why it's cool, where it came from, stuff like that.

"You know, hon, this could be the beginning. I could make a real business out of this, just like I was talking about last week. I want to cook real food for people, but more than that I want to *educate* them about a better way to eat.

Rox smiled at his enthusiasm. It was great to see him excited about something after the past two years of worry and frustration. But as she put her own nametag on to go to work, she felt reality pulling her back.

Luckily she didn't feel the same abhorrence for her employer's food that her husband did, since Smithson's was the sole source of their income at the moment. She harbored no illusions that they were doing anything more than just barely scraping by financially on what she made as a waitress, even when Jason's occasional catering jobs added to that.

"But babe," she tried not to sound like she was whining. "I don't see where we'll get the money for you to get started with something like that. I mean, you need equipment, brochures, advertising, supplies, lots of stuff, right? I like the idea, I do. I mostly like that *you* like the idea. But I don't get how it's supposed to happen."

"It wouldn't take *that* much money. At least, I don't think so. I guess I should put together some kind of start-up budgets and see what I'd absolutely need. But, still, there must be a way to do it," mused Jason as he kissed his wife goodbye and sent her off to the evening shift at the restaurant.

Even as he said it, though, he knew Roxanne was right. Here they were, living in Rox's parents' basement apartment because they couldn't even afford a place of their own. The sprawling new home they'd owned just a couple of years ago seemed light-years away.

His life had seemed so promising when he was first out of college, he could hardly believe that barely more than a decade later—when he should be in the prime of his blossoming career—he was barely making ends meet in an extraordinarily reduced lifestyle.

What was he thinking, that he could start up a new business? He must be crazy.

Jason rubbed at his temples as the now-frequent headache started throbbing again. He pulled his tee shirt over his head, swallowed a couple of aspirin, and headed out to his garden. He always felt a little better when he was puttering with his plants, thinking about the meals he would fix with the fruits and vegetables he was growing. Somehow just touching the living plants, nurturing them along, made everything in his miserable life seem a little less miserable.

—Chapter 3

"Drover. Come!" Marjorie called to her Australian cattle dog as she headed to the car. "Come on, Drover. In the car. Let's go to the dog park!" as she snapped her fingers at the open door of her Subaru.

Drover stopped scratching at the tennis ball that was hiding just under the edge of the bush and jumped eagerly into the car, wagging his backside. She didn't like that his original owners had docked his tail, but she *did* find it endearing when his tail-end wiggled, seemingly without his conscious intention, revealing his happiness. Marjorie had said the magic words, "dog park, " and he was ready to go!

Although she had a large fenced yard, Marjorie liked to give Drover the chance to play with other dogs so she tried to drive the ten minutes to the dog park at least once a week. It was a gorgeous summer day, clear and sunny and still cooler. The rainstorm two days ago seemed to have broken the heat wave they'd been having. She was glad the store schedule made it possible to be home early this afternoon and go.

It seemed that all the dog owners in town had the same idea and the parking lot was almost full. Marjorie eased into one of the only parking spaces, feeling grateful that it was generously shaded by the dense canopy of a sprawling maple. Someone must have just pulled out. Despite it getting on a bit in years, she loved her car, but in the summer she often wished it were white rather than the dark blue it actually was.

She left the windows open and tucked her water bottle into her tote bag, along with her book, two tennis balls, and three whole-wheat cranberry chocolate cookies they'd just baked at the café. It was to be their "little something extra" the following day and she hadn't yet had a chance to try one, although having created the recipe she felt sure they were good.

Drover ran enthusiastically into the park, wagging his tail end and exchanged sniffs and barks of greeting with the other dogs there.

Marjorie strolled slowly into the park, enjoying the day just as much as Drover, but in a quieter and more relaxed sort of way. The benches were nearly all filled with other dogs' humans, so she meandered across the park to the only empty one.

She watched Drover play, knowing that at some point she might need to go throw the ball for him but appreciating that, for the moment, he was in complete bliss just romping with his canine pals.

Marjorie took the cookie and studied it for a moment. It was a good-looking cookie, richly colored with the dark chocolate and full of glistening dried cranberries. She took a bite and chewed thoughtfully. Nice texture, subtle hints of orange, chewy dried cranberries, just the right sweetness. Good. *These will go over well. After we give them away tomorrow, we should add them to the café menu.*

Her cookie reverie was broken by a shadow falling over her. She looked up to see a tall, pleasant-looking man standing in front of her.

"Do you mind if I sit down?" he asked. "You seem a bit lost in thought and...well, I don't want to intrude."

She laughed lightly and easily and held out a cookie. "Please do sit down, and have a cookie. I'm a bit embarrassed to say that's the *deep thought* I was lost in—just analyzing the cookie."

"Are you a baker?" he asked as he took the cookie and sat down with an easy grace. He bit into the cookie and gave an appreciative "Ummm... that's *really* good."

Marjorie described her bookshop and café and the concept of "lagniappe"—a little something extra. "I think it's most meaningful to apply the concept more 'spiritually,' as in giving extra service, but I also like to apply it literally and we usually have a little 'something extra' that we give to customers. This happens to be tomorrow's *lagniappe.*"

She noted the man's warm brown eyes and

tousled graying hair. His eyes were clear, his skin smooth, and his body lean. He seemed younger than she suspected were his actual years. She thought he moved with the ease of someone who practiced yoga or tai chi.

"I'm so sorry," she exclaimed as she thrust out her hand. "I must've left my manners back in the car. I'm Marjorie Parker."

"Martin VanElton." He shook her hand and she noticed he had a nice grip, not too hard, and yet not trying to manipulate her into what she thought of as the "soft-girlie" handshake that some folks did without realizing it.

The two sat in companionable silence for a while, enjoying the sun, their cookies, and the fresh breeze that kept the day feeling cool.

A silky golden retriever bounded up to Martin, nuzzling his leg before sitting down patiently in front of him. "Meet Dearheart," he said to Marjorie with a smile.

"She walked up to our door one day at the farm and never left. My wife thought we shouldn't keep her— *couldn't* keep her—since she was certainly not some scruffy street dog. But we put ads out and flyers and asked around for weeks. No one knew anything about where she'd come from, so we finally stopped looking and just accepted that—however magically it happened —she'd chosen to live with us."

Marjorie scratched Dearheart behind her ears and realized with a bit of a shock that she was sorry to hear that Martin had a wife. *What is that about,* she wondered. *I'm not looking for a man!*

"Although we've got lots of land at the farm, obviously, Lynn always thought Dearheart needed to play with other dogs, so we've brought her here for years." He stopped and looked at Marjorie. "You've been coming here for a while? I'm actually a little surprised we haven't met before."

"With the business, I come whenever I can but there's no particular pattern since my hours can be all over the place. Probably just haven't been here at the same time." Marjorie scolded herself mentally for her brief dismay at hearing that Martin had a wife, a wife who obviously cared about dogs. "Maybe I've met Lynn before? Although I think I'd remember Dearheart. She's a really lovely dog!"

A cloud seemed to cross Martin's face. "Lynn's been gone now for nearly two years." A shudder of pain visibly passed through him. "Cancer."

"Oh, I'm so sorry." And she genuinely was. She was also startled to feel the slightest sense of relief. *Oh stop it, that's just sick. The man is still grieving for his wife, for God's sake. What is wrong with you?*

Those thoughts quickly passed, though, for she really could feel the weight of his grief. In fact, the next thoughts seemed initially as out-of-place to her as her initial interest in whether Martin actually was married or not. The feeling came to her, "There's something 'odd' about his grief."

Having only just met, she felt that pressing him further would be prying, but even as they moved back to lighter conversation, she was surprised that she continued to feel a sense of Martin being bothered by something beyond merely missing his departed wife.

She almost said something about *The Power of Acceptance*, how he might find it helpful, but had the same feeling as she'd had about asking any further questions. It seemed too soon, and she knew that trying to push the ideas on him when he wasn't ready—or he didn't know her well enough to trust her—could do more harm than good. *Too bad,* she thought, *I suspect it could help him with whatever is going on.*

The cloud that had passed over Martin seemed, on the surface, to pass and he and Marjorie talked easily for the next half-hour while their dogs played. She told him Drover had come to her as a rescue dog. First literally rescued out of the desert by a woman on horseback, then brought into her life when that woman's life changed and she could no longer keep him.

"I live alone, and quite happily so," she said with a smile, "but with Drover I never feel like I'm *really* alone. He might not be a great conversationalist, but he *is* great company."

The golden retriever came back over to nuzzle Martin's leg. He stood, saying, "Dearheart is saying it's time to go. I think the prospect of dinner has become an even stronger attraction than playing with her friends."

He shook Marjorie's hand. "I don't quite see why we haven't met before now, but I'll hope to run into you again." Coming out of another man's mouth it could sound like a "line" but from Martin it simply sounded like a genuine sentiment. She shook his hand warmly and replied, "Yes, I hope so."

She scratched Dearheart again under her chin. "And I hope to see *you* again, too." She watched Martin walk across the park and waved when he turned back toward her. *Nice*, she thought. *Nice man. And pretty dog.*

Marjorie pulled into her driveway and headed toward the back stairs with Drover. As she was unlocking her back door she heard her phone ringing. She grabbed it just in time, her breathless "Hello?" met by the familiar voice of her daughter.

"Mom," Sandy said, drawing the short word out into several syllables. "Where were you? I've been calling and calling."

"Sandy, honey, great to hear from you. Why in

the world don't you call my cell? I thought that's all you kids used today."

"Oh, Mom," she sighed affectionately. I just always feel like if I call you on your cell I'm interrupting or inconveniencing you."

"And making me run up the stairs to answer my land line isn't an inconvenience?" Marjorie made herself a glass of iced tea while they talked. It was such good-natured bantering, it almost took her breath away.

She still remembered the times, now more than a decade ago, when her relationship with Sandy wasn't this easy.

Almost fifteen years ago Sandy was just finishing up her MBA and entering the corporate world when Marjorie was making the decision to leave that same world behind. Marjorie had always thought it was a slightly odd role-reversal that her *child* was hassling her about being irresponsible and leaving her well-paying executive job for the uncertainties of starting Lagniappe.

When Marjorie chose to sell the house that Sandy had grown up in to obtain some of the capital she needed for the shop, Sandy had positively gone berserk. For years, in spite of Marjorie "knowing better" she just couldn't seem to keep herself from pushing back at Sandy, always trying to convince Sandy she was right, get Sandy to agree that it had been a good decision.

Perhaps not surprisingly, the harder Marjorie pushed, the harder it seemed that Sandy pushed back. Although Marjorie tried very hard to be clear that she was proud of Sandy for what she was accomplishing in her own career, somehow Sandy always seemed to hear reproach in everything Marjorie said, as though by Marjorie's choice to leave Maxwell Pharmaceuticals, she was invalidating the choices Sandy was making to embark on a corporate career.

Finally Marjorie had accepted that she needed to pay attention to what she was doing and simply allow Sandy to have her feelings, and allow *herself* to experience the sadness over their estrangement. She knew these principles and had applied them quite successfully in the early years of starting and growing Lagniappe, but she'd found it more difficult to *apply* when it came to Sandy.

She knew she was trying to *resolve* the resistance in Sandy, and as a result just experiencing more and more resistance, both *from* Sandy and in her own experience *of* Sandy. When she finally started listening to her own *state of being* instead of just working to change Sandy's mind, things almost immediately improved in their relationship.

Even now, as she chatted comfortably with Sandy, she took a moment to appreciate the ease and pleasure that had finally come to them.

"Mom, " Sandy was saying. "You sound unusually happy. Is something going on?"

Marjorie teased her in reply, "Now how is it that sounding 'happy' is something to cause suspicion, pray tell. Am I not *usually* happy?"

"Yeah, but there's something else. If it didn't sound so corny I'd say you have a 'lilt' to your voice that isn't normally there. You sure nothing's going on?"

Marjorie felt the slightest blush and held her cool iced-tea glass to her cheek. *Had meeting Martin actually brought a lilt to her voice, for goodness sake?* "Heavens, sweetie, nothing is *going on* as you put it." Deftly changing the subject, she continued, "Although I do have a program coming up at the shop I'm really excited about.

"Have you read *HomeGrown*?" she asked Sandy, "or heard about the movie? It's a documentary that's just being released."

"Funny, someone at the office was just talking about it—they were just finishing up the book and at lunch yesterday they were saying how interesting it was, but..." Sandy's voice became muffled, "I didn't hear enough of the conversation to get what it was actually *about.*"

"Are you eating something?" Marjorie asked, momentarily distracted by what she guessed were the sounds of her daughter chewing.

"Yeah, I finally got around to trying that cookie recipe you sent me recently, the one with the chocolate and cranberries. They're really excellent," as more munching sounded in Marjorie's ear. "Are you serving them in the café yet?"

"Speaking of funny, what funny timing," Marjorie laughed. "We just baked them up today and I was trying them out myself just a little while ago. We'll give them away for the next couple of days and then probably put them in the café next week."

"So, what were you saying about *HomeGrown*?" Sandy's voice was more distinct again, as though she'd either finished the cookie or thought better of trying to eat it and talk at the same time. "Some kind of program at the shop?"

"Yes, I'm really excited that we're sponsoring a showing of the movie next month."

"So, what's the story? It's a whole movie about gardening?" Sandy sounded a little skeptical that it would be all that exciting.

"Well, it does talk about gardening and farming, but that's only a tiny aspect of it. The idea of 'home grown' they're talking about, as I understand it, is more about globalization gone awry and proposing solutions that involve living a life more 'home grown' from the food we eat, the businesses we support, our relationships with our neighbors and families...."

Marjorie trailed off slightly. "I'm slightly embarrassed to say I haven't quite finished the book myself, although I've read enough of it, and enough other reviews of it, to feel confident that the movie has the chance to be very powerful.

"I had actually taken the book to the dog park with me today—that's where I was just coming from when you called—but I ended up meeting someone and talking the whole time rather than reading, so hopefully I'll finish it up when I go to bed tonight."

"Ah ha!" Sandy pounced. "Met someone, huh? I think *that's* probably the very thing I hear in your voice. Come on, what's up?"

"Sandy, I had a perfectly pleasant conversation with a perfectly pleasant man that I doubt I'll ever see again. That's hardly something 'going on.' Now just stop it." Her laugh took away any harshness of her words. "I need to get dinner going before it gets too late, so I'm hanging up now. Go finish your cookie and stop trying to make something out of nothing."

"I just want you to be happy, Mom. You and Daddy have been divorced forever. It would be nice if you had someone in your life, maybe even got married again. You're not getting any younger."

"Thank you, dear. I appreciate that." The slightest edge of sarcasm crept into her voice. "I'm not against the idea, it's just not my focus. I'm happy with my life, thank you very much. Now, really, I need to go and you surely have other more useful things to do than hound your mom about her love life.

"I love you. Talk to you again soon, sweetie."

"Bye, mom. Love you too."

Marjorie hung up the phone and began pulling salad ingredients out of her fridge. She'd been truthful with Sandy, she thought to herself. She was happy with her life.

Even so, as she added some cold grilled chicken to her salad and carried it to her dining room table, she found herself thinking, "Well, I wouldn't *really* mind it if I bumped into Martin again."

—Chapter 4

Dianne pulled her Lexus into the garage and sighed at the silver BMW left casually pulled off into the side parking spot. *Why, oh why, couldn't Chris put the damn car into the garage?*

Chris insisted that the car was ten years old and didn't need pampering, but somehow it still bugged Dianne. She shrugged her shoulders, determined to slough off a minor life annoyance *(no matter how recurring!)* and opened the glass door into the gleaming kitchen.

Chris was standing at the granite-topped island, pouring freshly brewed espresso over ice. "Want an iced coffee? We need to get dressed for dinner over at the Wilsons. Remember, everyone is supposed to wear black and white."

Grimacing slightly about the dress code facing them, Dianne accepted the tall glass of iced coffee and they headed down the hall to their dressing room. Chris already had clothes laid out, but Dianne stood for a long while staring into her closet. As she finally began pulling an outfit together, she told Chris about meeting Jay at work and her slightly revolutionary plans for their upcoming dinner party.

Chris looked at Dianne skeptically. "Do you really think anyone from Maxwell is going to care *at all* about this real food thing? I mean, you want to talk about real, let's be real here—they sure don't give a damn about people being healthy. They *need* people to be sick so that there's a steady market for their magic pills and potions. I'm actually surprised that *you* care."

"I don't know, somehow just listening to Jay talking today—seeing his passion for what he calls 'real food'—it just seemed like it would be a little something different than the usual dinner party. And, at least, we won't make people dress up any certain way." Dianne rolled her eyes, leaving no question how she felt about their friends' request.

"And, besides," Dianne continued, "I don't think that's fair about Maxwell! You know as well as I do that we make drugs that save a lot of lives. You make us all sound like such vultures. Might I remind you, too," as she glared pointedly at Chris's custom tailored black slacks, "that we enjoy a pretty comfortable lifestyle thanks to Maxwell Pharmaceuticals."

It was Chris's turn for eye rolling. "You know perfectly well that I'd be happy with a much simpler lifestyle. Please don't try to lay that on me. You *cannot* tell me that you think for one minute that Maxwell is all about doing good or helping people. Hell, most of their drugs just treat the symptoms that are side-effects from taking their *other* drugs."

Dianne sighed and turned her back to Chris. "Here, zip me up please." She knew there was no point in continuing this argument. They'd had it many times before, and she suspected would have it again. "Let's just forget it. We need to get a move on. Do you want to take your car or mine?"

Twenty minutes later they were nearing their friends' home. Perhaps surprisingly, the silence in the car had been comfortable, despite the earlier argument. They'd actually had that discussion so many times, Dianne didn't think either of them took it personally any more.

This time, however, while Chris drove, Dianne found herself thinking back to their conversation. She realized that she'd gotten so used to this particular argument, she didn't really *listen* any longer to what was being said.

If she allowed a little brutal honesty to creep in, it *was* true that an awful lot of their drugs really were used to treat "some symptom or other" which had pretty good odds of being a side-effect of some *other* drug the person was already taking. With the exception of a few antibiotics, very few of their drugs actually *cured* anything. And, of course, while the antibiotics unquestionably cured certain infections, they were increasingly understood to be vastly overused and create many other problems.

Is there a chance Chris might be right about Maxwell? She chased the thought away as quickly as it appeared. Dianne's entire career had been at Maxwell and she was proud of how successful she'd become there.

She was saved from her own thoughts by Chris. "Oh, I almost forgot to tell you. Michael called just before you got home."

"Michael?" Dianne sounded puzzled.

"Yeah, you know," Chris replied dryly. "Michael. Remember the hours of labor and then the emergency C-section you had twenty-six years ago? That was Michael. I know you work very hard and have a very important job, but I think he still expects you to remember who he is."

"Very funny," replied Dianne. "Michael is *also* the name of my boss, you will recall, and I couldn't think why *he* would be calling. I'm glad it was *our* Michael instead. What did he have to say for himself?"

"He was excited—he got the teaching job he really wanted at that progressive high school he was telling us about." Chris sounded rightfully proud.

Dianne on the other hand, let out a long sigh. "I know I should be happy for him, and of course in some way I am—I know it's the job he wanted—but I sure wish he'd picked a different field. I can just see him, twenty years from now, still living in his little student apartment since that's all he'll be able to afford. How is he *ever* going to be able to support a family on a teacher's salary?"

"Oh come on, Dianne. I know teaching isn't the highest paid job in the world, but plenty of teachers have families and live perfectly comfortable lives. I'm so proud of him that he stuck to his guns and is doing what he really wants to do!"

Chris turned into their friends' driveway and cut the engine. "Why can't you just be excited for him that he got the job he wanted. You know, success isn't *only* about the money. He's doing important work, not to mention work he really wants to do. Seems like a parent's dream for their son rather than one to bring about such heavy sighing."

"I know, I just worry about him, that's all." Dianne seized the opportunity to change the subject. "You'll never guess who I saw today. Do you remember Marjorie Parker from Maxwell? I can't believe it's been fifteen years since she left."

The pair walked toward the house and stumbled slightly as Dianne twisted the heel of her shoe. The Wilsons had a beautifully landscaped yard, but the cobblestone path that meandered up the deep front yard to the door was rough. Picturesque to look at, but treacherous to walk on, especially in high heels.

"Anyway," Dianne continued, hurrying to finish telling Chris about Marjorie before they got to the door and got swept into the party, "she owns that little bookshop down on Center Street. Lagniappe.

"You just wouldn't believe it—she says she's lost 50 pounds and she looks great. Really happy and relaxed. She also said she just got back from Costa Rica. Maybe we should think about going there on vacation sometime?"

Chris laughed. "Love, when was the last time you took a vacation?"

Dianne winced a little in response, but good-naturedly acknowledged, "Yeah, there is that." She smiled slightly at Chris. "Well, something to aspire to."

Just then the door opened and they joined the other black-and-white clad guests, saving any further discussion of Marjorie or Costa Rica until another time.

Although Dianne's regular coffee shop had reopened, she found herself heading back over to Lagniappe for her morning latte, intrigued to talk with Marjorie again.

Marjorie looked up from the display of books she was setting up when Dianne entered the shop. She took in her perfectly tailored suit, precisely draped scarf, classic high-heeled pumps and remembered a time when she had dressed the same way rather than the much more casual—and more comfortable—clothes that were appropriate for the shop.

Seeing Dianne brought back a flood of memories from her years at Maxwell and immediately made her grateful that she had left when she did.

At first she'd enjoyed her work there. She was good at her job and had been promoted quickly. At the time, the frenetic energy of the company had seemed exciting, but over the years the excitement waned and a more grinding sense of constant stress settled in.

Even so, it had been hard to leave the security—and the salary—but Marjorie had realized that she didn't want her life to just slip away from her, spending her years doing work she increasingly found to be more tedious, less rewarding, and just generally no fun.

Buying the shop had been a huge leap for her, but it had paid off—she made a comfortable living, loved going to work each day, even after all these years, and enjoyed the challenges of keeping her little shop thriving in an era where so many folks bought their books online.

She suddenly realized Dianne was looking at her oddly. "You look like you were a million miles away," she said.

Marjorie laughed. "Sorry, I guess I was. Seeing you just carried me back in a flash to my days at

Maxwell and my deciding to leave and start this shop."

"Yes, I'm sorry we didn't keep in touch better after you left. I had no idea this is even what you'd done."

Dianne paused a moment, not even thinking that what she said next might sound insulting. "You know, in all those years we worked together, I don't ever think I had you pegged as the entrepreneurial type." She remembered Marjorie as a quiet, dowdy number-cruncher who seemed perfectly satisfied to spend her days staring at her computer screen or poring over massive financial reports.

"Do you mind if I ask—did you quit *in order* to start this business or was it something that came up for you *after* you quit?" Dianne was surprised to hear herself ask the question since it hadn't even occurred to her to wonder until the words were out of her mouth.

Marjorie looked thoughtful. "I guess I'd have to say it was a little of both, if that makes sense." She paused again for a moment. "That is, I'd finally realized I was getting more and more miserable at Maxwell and that I wanted something completely different in the way of work. So you could say I did quit in order to start this business, but at the same time, I didn't really know what the particulars of the business would be until after I'd quit. I had more of a feeling about *how* I wanted the business to be than exactly *what* I wanted it to be."

She looked at Dianne and raised an eyebrow. "Why do you ask?" The next question popped out before she could stop it. "Are *you* thinking of leaving Maxwell?"

Dianne looked aghast. "Of course not!" she replied vehemently. "Why would you even think that?" Two bright spots of color formed on her cheeks.

"I was just wondering if you were asking about *my* leaving because you were considering the same thing. Sorry, certainly meant no offense." She could see that she'd upset Dianne and wondered why the simple question had bothered her so. *Maybe just a bit of "methinks thou doth protest too much"?*

Marjorie looked down at the display of books she had been setting up when Dianne had arrived at the shop and picked up one of the slim books. Holding it out to Dianne she said, "You know, you might enjoy this book. I discovered it about fifteen years ago and it's been one of my favorites ever since. This is a new printing and I thought I'd feature it as my special of the week. Buy one, get a second one free to give as a gift."

Dianne reluctantly took the book with its simple blue cover and glanced at the title. *The Power of Acceptance,* it said. *What the hell did that mean?* Didn't look like her kind of book, but she didn't want to be rude so she picked up a second one and said, "Okay, sounds like a good deal. I need to go back to the cafe and get a latte—can I just pay for them there or do I need to stop back up here at the main register?"

"Amber is in the cafe. She can take care of it all for you. And just tell her I said to ring the free one up as code #993. I don't have it set up in the computer yet."

"Great, thanks. I'd better get going. Lots going on at work and I'm going to be late."

Dianne stared at the stack of papers in front of her, piled high on her desk. It was the recap of the research reports on Maxwell's newest product.

They had just gotten the final FDA approval and everyone was excited about the sales potential of their latest wonder-drug. Or, as had been repeatedly pointed out in meetings, what was really exciting was the *profit* potential.

A small voice in Dianne's head nagged at her. *Isn't this exactly what Chris is always talking about? A drug that doesn't cure anything, one that the patient had to keep taking forever since if they stop taking it, the condition actually would get worse than it was before. A drug that treated a condition most people considered annoying but not medically dangerous.*

"Stop it!" Dianne was surprised to hear herself say out loud. She mentally silenced the voice in her head and went back to the business at hand. This was going to be a blockbuster product and her team's marketing plan would ensure that sales were great.

Hmmm, she thought, *maybe with my bonus I'll just buy a place in Costa Rica. I'll have to remember to ask Marjorie more about it.*

—Chapter 5

Marjorie glanced at her watch as she put away the last of her paperwork on her desk. Although she only barely admitted it to herself, it was no accident that she'd scheduled herself for the opening shift at the shop this morning, which meant she was ready to leave work at three that afternoon.

It had been exactly a week since she'd met Martin at the dog park and she thought it wouldn't hurt to be there around the same time today, just in case the Friday afternoon visit was a regular part of his schedule.

She scoffed to herself, even as she made plans to finish her work and head home to pick up Drover. *It's not like I'm really hoping to see Martin again,* she thought to herself, even as she acknowledged that yes, she actually did hope to see Martin again.

It was just as she'd told Sandy last week, she was absolutely content with her life and was not looking to add a relationship to it. *On the other hand...* she thought as she drove home, smiling slightly at the prospect.

Drover was more than willing to participate in her scheming and jumped happily into her Outback for the ride to the park. It was another gorgeous summer day, although hotter than last week had been, and Marjorie was again appreciative when she found one of the parking spots under the shade.

There were fewer people at the park than there had been the previous week and only about half the benches were occupied. A quick scan revealed that Martin wasn't sitting on any of them, so she settled onto an empty bench near the entrance to the park. *Someone must have just left,* she mused to herself. *This is prime real estate!* The bench was deliciously shaded by one of the park's sprawling maple trees, making it at least twenty degrees cooler than it was if you were sitting out in the sun.

She admitted to herself that she was more than just a little disappointed not to see Martin. Almost without thinking, she sat quietly on the bench and began her nearly-automatic routine of acceptance. *I accept that I'm experiencing disappointment right now, that's okay. I accept that I'm experiencing ambivalence right now, that's okay. I accept that I'm experiencing confusion right now, that's okay."* Her experience with acceptance reminded her that it was critical for her to keep her attention on the cause of her experience, the state of being, not on the effect—the fact that Martin wasn't there, and that she was confused about her desire to see him.

Marjorie watched Drover trot around the park,

wagging his tail-less backside happily. Since she was pretty sure that she hadn't seen Martin anywhere, she was startled to see a golden retriever that looked exactly like Dearheart. Sure enough, the dog trotted up to her, clearly remembering her from their meeting the previous week.

"Hi, sweetie," she greeted the blonde dog who was nuzzling at her thigh. She reached out to scratch Dearheart behind the ears, looking out over the park for a human partner for the gentle dog. "You can't be here alone, now."

To her surprise—and slight disappointment—she saw a young woman heading toward her, calling Dearheart's name. *Martin's girlfriend?* she wondered. Somehow, the way he'd sounded about losing his wife, she hadn't pegged him as having a girlfriend, much less one who looked to be about half his age.

The petite dark-haired woman caught up to Dearheart and gently chided her. "You know better than that, silly dog. You're supposed to *come* when I call you!"

She looked more closely at Marjorie and seemed to suddenly realize that Dearheart hadn't just wandered off, but had deliberately come to visit this pleasant-looking woman. Thrusting her hand out to Marjorie, she smiled and announced, "I'm Stephanie. Looks like you already know Dearheart."

Marjorie shook Stephanie's hand, noting that her grip was firm, her smile genuine, and her eyes bright. *Well, at least Martin has good taste*, she thought ruefully.

"I'm the farm manager," Stephanie continued. She looked at Marjorie with an open, quizzical expression. "How do you know Dearheart?"

"Oh, we just met last week. Martin and I shared a bench, so I got introduced to Dearheart in the process. I have an Australian cattle dog running around here, somewhere. Now, this one," she said, scratching under the retriever's chin, "is a real sweetie. She sure seems to live up to her name."

"That she does," Stephanie agreed. "Come on girl, we need to get back to work." She looked again at Marjorie. "Martin had been saying all day he planned on coming to the dog park this afternoon, so when he got hung up at work I offered to bring Dearheart over.

"It's funny—she's got all the room in the world to run around at the farm, but he seemed to really want to bring her today. So, here we are. But we do need to get back to work." She smiled again. "Well, I guess *I'm* really the one who needs to get back to work."

"Tell Martin I said hello, okay?" The words popped out before Marjorie could stop them, although she felt a little foolish, figuring Dearheart was probably much more likely to remember her than Martin was. Oh well, she'd already said it. "My name's Marjorie. Tell him Marjorie and Drover said hi."

"Sure thing." Stephanie walked off with Dearheart trotting alongside and Marjorie smiled to herself, recognizing the relief she felt that the younger woman appeared to simply be a colleague of Martin's, not a romantic interest.

Stephanie entered the farm office, opening her mouth to tell Martin about meeting Marjorie, but Martin held up his hand to silence her, motioning to the telephone at his ear. He was clearly on the receiving end of whatever conversation he was having.

She settled in to her desk across the room from Martin, half-listening to his end of the conversation which, after a long period of silence, and a few *um-hmm*'s mostly consisted of his saying, "Okay, as I've explained, it's not how we usually do it, but I'm going to go with it. Just call your order in at least two days ahead of when you need to pick it up so we can be sure we have everything you need." She felt like she'd probably missed the more substantial part of the conversation already.

Martin hung up the phone and turned to Stephanie. "Dearheart have fun at the park?" he asked. "You looked like you wanted to say something right when you walked in? Any problem?"

Stephanie was already buried in her own work and looked up with a puzzled expression. "What? Oh, no, everything was fine." She paused a minute, trying to remember what else it was she'd wanted to tell Martin. "Oh, I ran into a friend of yours, Marjorie? Never saw her dog, but she said she has an Australian cattle dog. She told me to tell you hello." Stephanie noted with some amusement that her boss looked pleased at her announcement.

In the five years she'd worked with Martin at the farm, she'd never seen him show the slightest interest in a woman. Well, other than his wife, Lynn, of course. She'd watched him go through the angst of her illness and eventual passing and he'd never seemed quite the same since then. She'd begun to think he would never get involved with another woman and she was surprised at the flicker of interest that she saw in Martin's eyes.

Martin quickly shifted back to business and reported on the phone call he'd been on when Stephanie had entered. "That fellow I was talking with on the phone is a new customer. He's got his first private chef job and managed to convince me to accept his order without a credit card."

He grinned and shook his head. "Not entirely sure how he did that, but there was just something so sincere in his voice, I found I wanted to help him. So, when he calls in his order—I think his catering job is in a couple of weeks—you can take it without the prepayment."

He passed a customer data form over to Stephanie. "Here's his info. He'll pay in cash when he picks the order up." VanElton Farms normally took credit card payment when an order was placed since setting the highly perishable food aside for one specific customer virtually guaranteed it would be wasted if the customer didn't follow through with picking it up. He hoped he wasn't making a mistake by promising this young chef he'd take his order without any payment guarantee.

Martin left the farm office a little after six and walked around the corner of the building to re-enter through the kitchen door. Although his home and the office were all in the same building, Martin liked to keep them physically separate.

Farming was enough of an all-consuming life already, and Lynn had insisted on doing whatever they could to turn their home into a small oasis *away* from the business. Every time Martin went outside just to come back inside, he felt like he was honoring Lynn in this small way.

He puttered around the kitchen, fixing a nice salad, reheating some of the zucchini casserole he'd made the previous evening, and grilling a beautiful lean buffalo steak to slice on top of the salad. He'd recently teamed up with a nearby farm raising all natural bison and he was enjoying trying out their different cuts of meat.

Before she got sick, Lynn had been the primary cook in their family, but he took over during those long months of chemo when she felt too weak to be in the kitchen and had taught himself to cook. He'd never be a great chef, but he truly enjoyed making good food, and after Lynn's passing he'd committed to himself that he was not going to slack off and eat fast food and pizza, but rather he would keep cooking for himself. After all, he was surrounded by top-quality produce and other ingredients. He had no excuse for not eating great food.

Although he did sometimes succumb to eating his dinner in front of the television, he tried to limit that particular bad habit and tonight he set a nice table and enjoyed his meal with a glass of wine. Given that there was no one available for dinner conversation, he read a few pages in the new book, *HomeGrown*, that he'd picked up the day before.

As a farmer, he'd wondered if the book was going to tell everyone they should be growing their own food, and he'd been intrigued to find the far-reaching application the authors proposed of a "home-grown" concept. It certainly was in sync with his own approach to his life and business.

He finished the last of his dinner and found himself staring blankly at the pages of the open book, *thinking* rather than *reading*. It started with the simple wish that Lynn could see the farm now and the improvements he'd made over the past couple of years.

As so often happened when he thought of his wife, he quickly descended into a spiral of negative thoughts. It wasn't just "grief." *That*, he recognized, *would be easier to deal with.*

He knew it didn't make rational sense, but thinking about Lynn inevitably made him angry. They had worked so hard throughout their years together to live well, eat right, maintain a positive attitude.

They'd met at a spiritual retreat and what had begun as a simple friendship—sympathetic strangers bonding over the challenges they were facing as they learned to quiet their minds and meditate—that friendship grew to a deep love, and they'd been happily married for nearly forty years.

They'd gone through a number of teachers and gurus over the years, a variety of approaches and practices, and while all had brought some benefit, none had prevented Lynn's body from being ravaged by the cancer that finally took her life. Wasn't she supposed to be able to heal herself? Or was it his job to heal her, and he'd let her down, again?

The ideas pummeled him, as they always did

when he made the mistake of stumbling down this dark path of thoughts. Even though his intellectual mind was more reasonable, there was an emotional side of him that felt they had failed. Their spirituality had been tested and they had failed miserably.

He'd already wrestled throughout his life with merging his strongly held spiritual beliefs with the idea of wealth. Although his parents had resented the struggles of their heritage, wishing—to no avail—that they'd been able to escape the farm and make a "normal living" at "normal" jobs, Martin felt deeply connected to the earth from the time he was a small child, and he'd been very happy to continue his parents' work at the family farm. His choice to emphasize his—and Lynn's—spiritual growth over financial abundance had seemed like the right choice in the early years.

But as the years went by, he knew that Lynn sometimes longed for a life with just a *little* more ease in it, a life that had the occasional luxury. Her abiding love for Martin kept it from being an open struggle between them, but his nagging sense of having failed her grew over the years.

Somehow her cancer seemed the tragic icing on the cake of a life gone wrong. All the meditating and chanting and praying and retreats and suffering the poverty of the devout didn't make a bit of difference—Lynn was still dead.

He opened his eyes wide, surprised to see the golden glow of the setting sun shining through the French doors into the kitchen. Martin shook his head, as though to shake away the cobwebs of painful thoughts. At least, he thought, there seems to be some small hope for financial improvement.

There seemed to be a growing awareness that food grown naturally, healthily, locally, and eaten in season was a good idea—both for the planet and for one's health—and he was seeing a corresponding increase in interest in his farm and its products. He knew there was more he needed to be doing, and hoped to figure it out eventually. Almost as though he could redeem himself in Lynn's eyes, if he could figure out how to stay true to himself *and* make a decent living.

He wondered, as he often did, if she could see him, see what was going on at the farm, if she still *existed* on some plane. He believed she did, and sometimes even felt as though she were there with him, especially out in the fields, working alongside him as they had for so many years.

"I hope you know, baby, I'm trying, I'm really trying," he said softly as he put his dinner dishes away. He wasn't even sure what that meant to him, but he knew it was important that she know that.

—Chapter 6

Jason stared at the menu he'd written out in his angular handwriting, nodding his head slightly. It was good.

After his quick assurances to his new client that he could, *of course,* prepare an appropriate meal for her dinner party, he discovered that the quest for the perfect menu was harder than he'd anticipated.

He also knew that there was no such thing as the *perfect* menu, given how varied everyone's taste was, but he did want to be sure that what he sent to Dianne represented the ideals he'd espoused to her— real food, focused on seasonal ingredients, as much as possible grown or produced locally, and obviously delicious.

From his research about the business of being a personal chef, he knew there was computer software for managing menus, recipes, inventory and the like, but he knew he couldn't afford any of that. Yet. Luckily he actually liked keeping hand-written notes in his old leather-bound notebook.

He looked at his menu again, one last time before emailing the proposal to the client. *Yes,* he nodded to himself again, *it's good.* He opened his old laptop and typed out a quick note to Dianne with the menu and a request for fifty-percent deposit up-front. He knew that was standard so he felt fine asking for that, but he did worry a little about where the rest of they money would come from to buy what he needed.

If he only had a little bit of start-up capital he would *own* the things he needed and not have to buy them for each job as it came up, which sure ate into any potential profit. And he'd be able to buy his food at better prices, too.

Jason looked up at Roxanne who had been folding laundry. "Thanks for doing that, hon," he said to her as he nodded at the piles of folded clothes. "I know that's *my* job, but I sure want to get this menu sent over to Dianne this morning."

He gave her a wry half-smile. "Well, what I really want to do is get the menu to her and get her deposit payment. Then I'll know the job's for real, and also I can start buying what I need." He paused, hesitating before continuing.

"You know, hon, it's possible I won't really make any money off this one job. There's so much I need to buy that I don't have." The defeated look crept back into his face.

Roxanne leaned over and gently touched his hand. "But, babe, if this goes well, who knows... it could lead to other things that *would* make money. And I have to say I really love seeing you excited about something for a change." She had hated seeing her bright, warm, enthusiastic husband sink deeper and deeper into despair over these past two years.

When he'd first lost his job, they'd both assumed he'd find another, even if it took a few months. But as the months went by and turned into years, they'd both lost hope. Losing their house to the bank had been devastating although she was grateful that her parents had this apartment in their basement so at least they weren't homeless and didn't have to pay rent.

With that assistance, they were scraping by on her waitressing earnings and his occasional catering job, but it had been hard. And the hardest part was watching the light go out of her husband's eyes. She felt like she was seeing at least a tiny glimmer of it now. So even though this private chef idea he had seemed a little far-fetched to her, she'd realized it was the happiest he'd looked in a long time and she wanted to support him.

Jason had clicked "send" just before he and Rox had started talking so he was surprised to hear his computer chime, announcing the arrival already of Dianne's reply. He let out a deep sigh of relief when he read her email accepting the menu and saying he could come right over to the office and get the cash for the deposit if he wanted. Cash. *Excellent*, he thought. That was even better than having to deposit a check and wait for it to clear.

As Jason walked out to his truck, he waved at his next-door neighbor who was pulling weeds from the narrow strip of garden that separated their driveways. She called out a cheery "Hello!" to him and was pleased to see that he looked much more upbeat than usual.

She always seemed so friendly to him, Jason felt that his wave back to her seemed almost inadequate, so he stepped over to the picket fence between their yards to chat for a moment. Getting that cash deposit could wait for five minutes.

"You know," he offered, "if you put down a good layer of mulch after the plants are well up, you won't have to weed so much."

She laughed. "Oh, I know. Every year I *mean to* do that, and somehow I find myself out here yanking weeds in the sun. Then I think that after I get *these* weeds pulled, I'll put down that mulch but it still doesn't happen. I'm beginning to think that I secretly like weeding." She smiled warmly. "Your garden is doing well," she said admiringly with a nod towards his raised beds.

"Yeah, things are coming along. I got some things in a little late, though, which is a bummer since I have a catering job in a couple of weeks and I'd love to use some of my veggies, but I don't think what I need will be ready yet. I'll have to buy them."

"Catering job?" she said with a confused look. *I thought he was some kind of executive, not a caterer*, she thought to herself. "Tell me about that."

Jason gave a short version of how his being a personal chef for Dianne's dinner party came about and said that he was headed to the client's office now to pick up the deposit money. He found himself telling her that he was worried about where he'd get the rest of the money to buy what he needed, explaining that final payment wouldn't be due until after the event, by which point he would have already had to spend way more than just the fifty percent deposit.

"Well, if you get in a bind, let me know," she said. "I've known your in-laws for years and I'd be glad to lend you the money." She surprised herself by making the offer, but at the same time she was glad she'd done so. *How else does someone like that ever get a break, a chance for a fresh start?*

Jason looked as surprised as she felt and stammered out his thanks. As he backed his old pick-up truck out the drive she looked after him and realized she didn't actually even know his name. *It's a little late to formally introduce myself now*, she mused. *I must remember to ask Walt and Louise.*

Jason parked in one of the "visitor" slots in front

of Maxwell Pharmaceuticals and looked around at the elaborate building, exotic landscaping, and towering waterfall that flanked their sign. *No wonder our drugs cost so much*, he thought ruefully to himself as he locked the truck and headed in to meet Dianne.

"Jay!" Dianne greeted him enthusiastically. "I love the menu. And your price seems very reasonable."

Aww, hell, he silently kicked himself. *That means I probably didn't charge enough.*

After he went over the menu with her just to be sure they were all clear on what each dish was and how it would be served, Dianne pulled her purse out from under her desk and counted out a stack of bills. He marked his email she'd printed out to indicate she'd paid half the total as a deposit and put the money in his wallet appreciatively.

As the elevator dropped back down to the lobby, though, his appreciation seemed to drop as well and by the time he was sitting in his truck again, the bitterness that had come to be his near-constant companion was back. *I'll bet she never has to wonder if she'll have enough money to buy groceries with.*

In an effort to shake off the gloom that had settled around him, Jason pulled into the small parking lot on Center Street and headed into Now You're Cooking, the little shop that was full of wonderful cooking gear and exotic ingredients. As an antidote to his bad mood, it only partly worked since for all the pleasure he got at wandering the aisles and admiring the gleaming merchandise, there was the steady voice in his head reminding him that he couldn't afford to buy most of it.

As he walked back to the parking lot, he noticed a poster in the window of the shop next door announcing a special showing of the documentary *HomeGrown*. He'd caught a bit of the buzz about the popular book that had been made into a film, but hadn't yet read it. The words "local and sustainable food" on the poster caught his eye and he stopped to read it more carefully.

Hmmm....sounds interesting. And it's free, even better. He noted the date and thought maybe with a couple of weeks notice like this, Roxanne could get the night off.

He realized he wasn't even sure what store window he was looking in, so he backed up a bit to better see the sign. *That's right,* he thought. *This is Lagniappe. I remember coming in here once, years ago. Nice shop.* He thought about celebrating his catering job by splurging on a fancy coffee drink inside at their cafe, but caught himself as he remembered that every penny and then some of that deposit in his pocket was going to be needed.

The bitterness sank back around him as he remembered how carelessly he'd spent money on designer coffee just a few years ago. Hadn't given it a thought at the time. And he was pretty sure that Lagniappe's coffee wasn't nearly as expensive as that Starbucks next to his old office that he used to frequent.

Once again reminded of how far he'd fallen, Jason slid behind the wheel of his battered old truck, swallowed a couple of aspirin for the headache that was starting up again, and headed for home.

—Chapter 7

Jason pulled up to the rambling farmhouse and wondered for a moment if he was at the right place. It looked more like someone's home than a business, but then he saw the "VanElton Farms" sign off to the left. Once he noticed the entry door and large storefront style windows on that ell wing, he realized that must be the farm office and showroom and the rest of the house probably really was the home for the farmer's family. He parked his truck in a shady spot and headed in to pick up his order.

Martin looked up as the door opened and wondered if this was their new customer, the personal chef that had somehow talked him into taking his order without a credit card payment. Although the farm store was open to the public, relatively few strangers actually just wandered in so he wasn't surprised when the young man introduced himself and said he was there for his order.

Martin went into his cool room and came out with a flat crate of freshly picked produce. "We were able to get eggplants, onions, and zucchini that have at least some parts of them that are about the same diameter, just like you asked," as he pointed out the various vegetables. "I'm just curious, what are you going to do with them that that's important?"

"I'm making a grilled veggie Napoleon as one of the courses for this dinner, and if I can stack up slices of the vegetables that are around the same size it just makes it look better. I'll just use all the parts that are too big or too small to make something else with for another time. A ratatouille or something."

Martin pointed out the pile of small cucumbers. "These Diva cukes are great when they're small like this. They're seedless, there's no bitterness, just a great 'cucumber-y' flavor. What are you making with them?"

"I'm doing a creamy cucumber soup with dill and mint. Kind of an up-dated classic, great for a hot summer's evening."

The pair kept talking their way through the crate of vegetables, with Martin pointing out special features of his produce and prodding Jason into telling more about his plans for the dinner party.

Jason opened up as they talked and Martin found himself sympathetic to the young man. "Got a few minutes?" he asked. "Would you like to see around the farm?" He stuck his head through the door into the farm office behind them and asked Stephanie to keep an eye on the front, and they walked out into the clear sunny day.

Although this was the first time they'd met, the two men fell into an easy camaraderie as they strolled around the nearer sections of the farm, Jason talking about his own small gardening efforts and Martin describing the changes the farm had gone through since his parents' time.

Jason shared more of how his interest in real food and sustainable agriculture had unfolded as a result of the time on his hands after he was laid off. Martin could feel his very genuine enthusiasm for food, his respect for the ingredients, his interest in helping others to learn as he had, but as they talked the bitterness that had become Jason's regular companion crept back in. Martin could feel his despair as almost palpable energy.

They arrived back at the farm office and Jason paid for his order from the cash Dianne had given him. He counted out almost all of the money from her deposit and scowled as he thought of everything he still had left to buy.

"Anything wrong?" Martin asked, puzzling over the look that had come over Jason's face.

"Nah," Jason replied sourly. "Everything's fine. It's just that I've still got a lot more food to buy, some equipment I need, and I've used up almost all of my client's deposit. Where the hell the rest of the money is coming from, who knows."

He shrugged his shoulders and picked up the insulated bag that held his bison tenderloins. Martin offered to carry out the flat crates of produce and silently they put everything in the back of Jason's battered pick-up.

Despite his obvious worries, Jason regained control and held his hand out to shake Martin's. Sincerity and gratitude thickened his voice as he thanked him. "I know you said you don't normally hold an order without a credit card so I really appreciate your help, man. It's bad enough to just barely have the cash to pay you, but would've been so much worse if I'd been scrambling and scratching trying to find all this stuff at the last minute from different vendors. And you really do have the best looking produce I've seen around. Plus the bison." He stopped for a minute to clear his throat. He shook his head slightly and said, "Just, thanks."

Martin watched him drive off, feeling strangely disquieted by their encounter.

Marjorie parked her car at the dog park, wishing for one of those shady spots she'd been so lucky to get recently. The thought crossed her mind again that she should consider getting a white car instead of this blue. Of course, conversely, the way the dark car warmed up in the winter-time sun was most welcome in January.

As Drover bounded ahead of her, she felt an unmistakable lift as she saw Martin sitting on a bench just ahead of them. *Oh, all right,* she said to herself, smiling. *He's a nice man and I enjoy seeing him. What's the big deal.*

She sat next to Martin and offered him a brownie. She waited, expectantly, as he bit into it and looked unusually pleased with his appreciative, "Ummmm...."

"We're trying out something new," she reported grinning. "It's a 'raw' brownie—all natural ingredients, no flour or anything, and not cooked at all. Pretty good, huh?"

He looked inquisitively at the piece remaining in his hand. "It's *really* good." He turned it over again and then thoughtfully ate it. "Raw? Seriously, not cooked?"

"Yes, I'm actually a big believer in the whole *middle ground* sort of approach to life, and personally I like too many foods to take an all-raw approach to eating, but I still think it's interesting to open folks' minds a little to what's possible. So we try to offer a variety of things for our *lagniappe*—some traditional cookies and sweets, some *alternative* things like this, and certainly some things that aren't edibles at all. This recipe is a particular surprise since it tastes just plain yummy!" She smiled as she said "yummy" and popped a piece into her own mouth.

After finishing the chocolate-y goodness of the

brownies, the two sat in companionable silence for a bit, then began chatting loosely about the weather, their dogs, their respective businesses. As their conversation continued, Marjorie kept noticing that Martin seemed distracted, not fully *with* the conversation.

"Everything okay?" she finally asked. "You seem a little...." She trailed off, not sure that she knew him well enough to make such an observation.

Martin shrugged slightly, but didn't deny the claim. "I think it's just this new customer I met today. I can't seem to get him—or, more accurately, his *situation* —out of my mind."

He went on to tell her about Jason, describing his obvious and genuine enthusiasm but how he seemed so overwhelmed with discouragement, even now on what seemed to be the edge of an exciting new venture.

"I just can't help thinking things would go more easily for him if he had a more positive outlook," he said. "Not that I could say anything like that to him. I barely just *met* him."

"I know what you mean," Marjorie replied thoughtfully, "although I find I have a slightly different take on that idea than some do." She paused briefly, wondering if she should continue. The timing seemed right, so she plunged on ahead.

"So often it seems that people try to force themselves into positive thinking, squashing down what they're actually experiencing—their actual feelings of worry, concern, fear, uncertainty and so on. They put on a happy face even when it's not what they're really experiencing and then they wonder why things don't seem to be working out for them, despite their positive thinking." She marked off the words "positive thinking" by making quotation marks in the air with her hands.

"I know I used to do that myself. Years ago I had read a number of books about positive thinking and the law of attraction and tried to *make* myself be positive, even when it wasn't what I was feeling. I felt like I needed to *resist* things that I didn't want and *force them* to change through my acting positive. After all, it seems so counter-intuitive to *accept* things you don't want.

"It took me a while to understand the difference between accepting how you feel—that is, the state of being you're experiencing—and accepting the actual circumstance or outcome of that state of being. And it took even longer to understand that it was only through accepting your state of being could you actually *change* that outcome."

She saw a flicker of comprehension in Martin's eyes and a look of open curiosity on his face, so she hesitantly pulled a copy of *The Power of Acceptance* from her tote bag. "This little book really helped me a lot. It's straightforward, has some simple practices to help you *get it*, and really just made the whole thing click for me. It might sound a little bit like a cliché, but this book literally changed my life." She handed it over to Martin. "I just had the feeling this afternoon to bring it to you. I hope you don't mind."

He took the slim volume from her and turned it over, half listening to Marjorie and half reading the back cover. "It sounds intriguing. Let me pay you for it."

She shook her head. "No, thanks for offering, but I want you to have it. It's a gift." She smiled warmly. "I don't know if it'll change your life like it did mine, but I do think you'll find it interesting."

She stood up and called Drover. "I need to get going. Hope you enjoy the book."

Martin thanked her again as she headed off to her car. She looked back at him just before driving away and saw that he was sitting there reading. She smiled to herself. Somehow she had the feeling this might help him.

—Chapter 8

The day of Dianne's dinner party dawned sunny and bright, foretelling of a typical hot summer day. Jason woke up just as the sun came up, eager to get going with his work, equal parts excited and scared. He hoped his belief that he could do this would be proven true!

He knew he could cook each of the dishes in the menu he'd prepared and it would be delicious. And he knew that he could speak to Dianne's guests about the ingredients and about the whole concept of "real" food.

But he had to admit, if only to himself, that cooking for the ten people at the dinner—as distinct from cooking for the two of them as he usually did, or maybe six when they'd had friends over—and keeping the timing right did make him just a bit nervous. Okay, he thought, a *lot* nervous.

Roxanne rolled over in bed and squinted in the morning sun at her husband. It was definitely not normal for him to be out of bed and dressed at this ungodly hour. At least it seemed ungodly to her, having worked last night until closing time and then stayed late to get things set up for today as a partial repayment to her co-worker who was taking her shift today.

"What's up, babe?" She looked at the clock and back again at Jason. "Pretty early...."

"Oh, I know, I'm just excited about the job today." He grinned, ruefully. "Okay, excited and a little jittery. Thought I'd just get a start on the final planning and so on. I know I can't show up at her house this early, but there's lots I can still do here."

Roxanne rolled over, away from the sunlight streaming in through the window. Her muffled voice came out from under the covers. "Let me know when I can help. Sounds like this first part is maybe just on your own." She was hopeful that last statement was true and was relieved when Jason planted a kiss on top of her head.

"You sleep a while longer. I definitely have some stuff to do by myself."

Three hours later, a well-rested Roxanne came out to the patio where Jason was just finishing up his detailed work-flow sheets for the job. He smiled at her, looking more at ease than he had several hours before.

"Okay," he said, gathering up his trusty leather notebook and a stack of loose papers. "I'm ready to tackle this thing. Wish I could've been doing actual food prep ahead of time, but that's gotta all happen in the client's kitchen. But I really think I've got it so well planned out in terms of what to do when that it will go really smoothly."

He glanced down at his watch. "Good timing, too. It's just about the right time to show up at Dianne's and get started."

Chris answered the door after Jason rang the bell and offered to help carry in his supplies. Jason found Chris immediately easy to be with, relaxed and helpful without getting in the way and the two chatted amiably as Jason got organized for the day of cooking.

"Dianne tells me this is your first personal chef job?" Chris asked with interest. "What made you decide to go into this field?"

Jason was usually sensitive about telling strangers how he'd lost his job and hadn't been able to find another—even in these tough economic times he couldn't help but feel it as a personal failure—but found himself opening up easily to Chris. He explained how he'd found cooking to bring him a sense of productivity and he discovered he had a knack for it. After all the negative feelings that being jobless had created, the satisfaction from cooking a good meal that was enjoyed by others was rewarding.

Chris listened intently. "Dianne also said that you were going to focus on so-called *real food*? She's asked you to speak to the guests about the dishes, why they are special, where the food came from, stuff like that?"

Jason couldn't help but notice a slight air of skepticism to Chris's questions. "You don't think that's a good idea?" he asked Chris, wondering what sort of mess he might have gotten himself into.

"Oh, no, I think it's a great idea. I just wouldn't have imagined that *Dianne* thought it was such a good idea. You must have been pretty persuasive when you talked with her."

Jason shook his head slightly. "Actually, I didn't say all that much. It just seemed to unfold as we talked. It is something I've become a bit passionate about, so I hope you all like what I'm fixing and how the presentations go. You don't think Dianne will regret having asked me to do this do you?"

Chris patted Jason reassuringly on the shoulder. "I'm sure it will work out fine. I'd better leave you alone and let you get your job done."

Roxanne arrived about an hour before the guests and was relieved to see that everything seemed under control in the kitchen. It helped that Dianne and Chris had a huge kitchen with what seemed like miles of counter space and commercial-type appliances, so between their professional set-up and Jason's meticulous planning, the day had gone smoothly.

Beyond that brief visit with Jason when he first arrived, neither Chris nor Dianne had set foot in the kitchen all day, but Dianne did pop in just after Roxanne arrived so that they had a chance to consult on the table setting and service plans. Just then, Melanie— their other server—showed up and everything cranked into high gear.

Jason laid out the plates and simple crystal bowls for the chilled soup, thankful again for the miles of counter-space in Chris and Dianne's kitchen. Even at that he bumped into a pile of their papers and personal stuff at the end of the stretch of counter that he needed. He carefully stacked things together and moved them out of the way, holding down the stack with a book that he found sitting there.

He couldn't help but notice the title, *The Power of Acceptance*, and wondered what *that* meant. The book looked brand-new so he handled it especially carefully, drying his hands well first. Curiously, he flipped it over to read the back jacket.

"Acceptance is your natural state," it declared, "and acceptance opens you up to allowing in all the good that is yours. It's all there, ready for you, but as long as you're resisting, there's no room for it to come to you."

Seriously? He shook his head slightly. *I should've just accepted that my life would turn to crap after I lost my job?* He plunked the book on top of the stack of papers and turned away. Even as he did so, though, the next thought came in less invited. *Yeah, but you've been so pissed off and tight and stressed all this time, too, that doesn't seem to have especially helped either.* He paused briefly.

And, you know, after you let go a little of the anger and allowed yourself to use this time to learn something new—like about cooking and real food—life actually has been better, and you even got this gig, without fighting for it or even really looking for it.

He deliberately switched off the train of thoughts in his head, knowing he needed to focus on the task at hand. But he also knew as he did so that there might be something to that book after all. What was it called? Maybe he'd see if the library had it.

Rox and Melanie each carried trays with four servings of soup and carefully placed them in front of the guests. Jason took the final two in, setting one each in front of Dianne and Chris at either end of the long, elegantly set table. He looked around at the guests who looked back at him, slightly puzzled that he was still standing there.

You can do this, he said firmly to himself. *It's just talking about something you feel passionate about to a handful of people.*

He zeroed in on one friendly looking woman in the middle of the group and smiled at her. "Good evening." He nodded around the table at their bowls of chilled soup. "Please, don't let your food get cold. Eat." He was glad to see that the sympathetic-looking woman he'd chosen as his "anchor" smiled at his little joke.

"Dianne has asked me to tell you just a little bit about each dish you'll be eating tonight, and also how I've made you a meal that focuses on real food, as local as possible, with simple, but—I hope—delicious preparation.

"It's been a hot day, so your first course is a fresh update of an old classic. It's a cool and refreshing cucumber soup. Notice how it actually tastes like cucumber. These are fresh, locally grown, picked just yesterday, a type of cuke grown for its great flavor, not just because it transports well. There's a slight bite of garlic and spicy pepper, with the cooling fresh summer herbs of dill and mint. All grown locally, blended with a rich creamy Greek yogurt, also made from local milk from pastured cows. Enjoy."

He nodded at Dianne, noting happily that she had already almost finished her soup, and slipped back into the kitchen to be sure Rox and Melanie were plating the next course the way he wanted.

He'd come up with this stacked roasted summer vegetable napoleon last summer to use some of the abundance from his own garden and had perfected how he thought it should look. Rox knew it almost as well as he did and had worked with Melanie to make sure the plates were picture-perfect.

Again he carried the last two plates in for Dianne and Chris. He felt more at home this time and chose a different guest to be his anchor. This fellow looked a little more challenging and Jason found himself enjoying the chance to—just maybe—open this guy's eyes a bit.

"We're moving from that cool soup to something a little heartier, but still keeping with summertime. It's all fresh local veggies, grilled but served at room temperature so you won't overheat! And here's an area —just one of the many—where *you* can choose where you want to fall on the real-slash-local food spectrum.

"See those two lovely slices of fresh mozzarella there? You could simply choose to buy the mozzarella over at the Costco and you'll actually get a decent product. But it won't be locally made, of course. Or you could decide that you wanted to *focus* on local, but not try to be *exclusively* local, and you could buy a gorgeous imported Italian buffalo milk mozzarella from the cheese specialty shop. Or you could even do like I did and *make* your own mozzarella from fresh local milk."

He saw several of the guests looking surprised— and impressed—at his announcement of his freshly made cheese. *Little do they know how easy it is*, he smiled to himself.

"And it's all good. Some folks, of course, take an all-or-nothing approach but for me, I think it doesn't need to be that extreme, unless you really feel called to that. Even small changes can be improvements. I'm not here to preach to you or try to convince you of anything particular. I just hope that by enjoying a lovely meal of great local fresh food, you might appreciate the possibilities." He smiled again as he headed back to the kitchen. He felt good. It was going well.

He had carefully slow-roasted the lean bison tenderloin, which he now sliced into tender medallions and topped with a rich blackberry port sauce. The new potatoes had been steamed earlier and now liberally brushed with garlic butter, finished off on the grill pan, smashed into rustic rounds, and then topped with an herbed sour cream.

The salad was a simple mix of fresh baby greens, with slivers of fresh grilled peaches and blue cheese. He looked at the plates proudly, all lined up on the counter ready to be carried to the waiting guests. The tension and worry that woke him up so early seemed long in the past. The food was good, he knew it from the empty plates and enthusiastic comments coming back from the table.

He had a sudden flash of himself about three years ago, before the threat of losing his job had even entered his consciousness, before it had ever occurred to him that he would learn to cook, much less learn to *care* so much about food, and he laughed. That person, the one he'd spent so much of the past two years trying to find again, suddenly seemed like a faraway stranger, and not a very likable one at that.

Rox looked at him oddly and he realized that he actually had laughed out loud. "No worries, hon. Just happy it's going well."

The rest of the dinner passed by in a blur. Jason was aware that it went well, but he was so tired by the time they finally finished serving and cleaning up that he could hardly think when Dianne sought him out in the kitchen. Melanie had already gone, and Jason and Roxanne were polishing the stainless appliances, just ready to leave. Everything had been packed up and the kitchen was spotless.

Dianne handed him an envelope. "Great job, Jay! The whole meal was amazing and that berry mousse was perfect for dessert. Light as air but so much flavor and just right after a big meal. Here's the balance due and something extra for you and your crew. It really was wonderful, thank you so much." She looked almost teary-eyed. "I will admit that before tonight I'd had a few moments of thinking that I'd lost my mind, having you do this." She realized how that might sound and smiled warmly.

"No offense, of course. I just mean that this isn't

the *obvious* crowd for this thing. One of my colleagues, in fact, did comment that if everyone ate like this and got so much healthier, maybe it would put us out of business." She smiled again, wondering if just maybe that might be partly true.

"Be sure to give me some of your business cards. I wouldn't be surprised if you got other business from some of these folks."

Jason mumbled apologies that he didn't have cards with him, knowing that of course he actually didn't have cards at all since that, along with everything else, was an investment that he just hadn't been ready yet to make when they were barely able to pay their bills.

He sat in the car a moment while Roxanne buckled her seat belt, feeling a strange mixture of pride that he'd successfully done it and frustration that he'd basically done it all for about two dollars an hour for his labor after he considered all his expenses.

"Well done, babe!" Roxanne congratulated him.

"Yeah but I think we lost money!" he snapped back at her.

She lost her smile. "What are you talking about? She just gave you a huge tip!"

He looked defeated. "I know and I didn't mean to snap at you. Sorry." He shook his head. "It's just that to do a 'one-off' job like this when I don't have the equipment I need, I have to rent stuff, I have to buy all my food at retail, buy basic stuff like a chef's coat—well there sure isn't much profit left to put in the bank. If only I had a little start-up money to get things going. Then a job like this would actually help pay the bills!"

Jason pulled his battered truck in at Martin's and parked under the shade tree again. His air conditioner was only blowing hot air this morning, so the shade was all the more welcome.

Martin looked up when Jason came in. "How'd it go?" he asked with genuine interest. He'd been intrigued with the younger man's plans for the dinner.

"Really well, in fact. Thanks. The food turned out great, the guests seemed to like my little presentations on each course, and the client gave me a big tip." He grinned. "Which I'm here to spend."

Martin grinned back at him. "Okay, sounds good. What's the occasion this time?"

"I want to recreate the meal for my in-laws tonight. They may drive me crazy now and then, but they've been really, really good to me and my wife and it seems like a good way to say thanks." He hesitated a moment.

"After I lost my job a couple of years ago, they've been so supportive, both emotionally and *literally* since we moved into this nice apartment they'd made in their basement. They won't let us pay rent, insisting that any month we have enough money to afford rent, we need to put that money instead into savings so that someday if I do get a job, or get this business going, or whatever, that we'll at least have some money to put the deposit down on a real place to rent. Of course, it seems like we never have enough money to do that, so I guess it's a good thing they're not charging rent."

He was usually too embarrassed to tell anyone that and he looked at Martin expecting to see pity or disgust at Jason's failings. Instead he saw a flicker of admiration.

"You know," Martin said thoughtfully, "I've been wondering whether there's any chance that you'd want to come work for me? It would be just part-time and probably doesn't pay a huge amount at first, but I think it could grow. In money, that is. You could keep it part-time if you wanted to continue to develop your personal chef business."

Jason looked interested so Martin continued. "In a sense, what I need is someone to do what it sounds like you did last night for those dinner guests, but to local restaurants. Help them see why it's smart to buy local, sustainable food." He paused. "Preferably from VanElton Farms, of course!"

Jason found himself nodding along as Martin spoke. "Yes, I think that could be really interesting. It was fun talking about the food last night and I wouldn't be surprised if some of those folks became your customers, actually. I'd want to talk it over with my wife, but, yes, I'd say I'm interested. Can I have a couple days to get back to you?"

Martin agreed and handed over the bags of produce and another bison tenderloin to Jason. "Enjoy your dinner tonight and we'll talk more soon."

As Jason drove away he found the idea growing on him. It would be great to actually be earning some money again, even if it wasn't a lot to start with. And doing work he really believed in.

And besides, he smiled to himself, *I'll bet I get a discount on the food I buy.*

—Chapter 9

Marjorie was excited that tonight was the screening of *HomeGrown* at Lagniappe. She'd been intrigued by the book and had heard only good things about the documentary film. Ordinarily she'd have previewed the film before she even booked the event or at the very least checked it out before the public showing, but the timing just hadn't worked out. She hoped she wasn't making a mistake, but she felt confident. Her gut told her it would be great.

Marjorie had designed Lagniappe from the beginning with an eye toward holding public events. She felt strongly about creating community and having her shop be more than simply a place that sold things.

She'd never been sorry that she'd invested the money in her movable display shelves. They were pricey compared to simple built-ins but it meant she could rearrange the shop at will including opening up a big area adjacent to the cafe and end up with quite a lot of seating.

That meant rather than having to have a large special events room that sat empty most of the time, she only needed a much smaller space in which to store the furnishings that weren't being used at the moment —usually the extra chairs for the additional seating or the cafe tables when turning the cafe into seating area. Much better use of her square-footage, she knew.

She heard her name being called and looked up to see Allison coming toward her. "Can I help you get things set up?"

"Hey, thanks," Marjorie smiled appreciatively. "Normally the rest of my staff takes care of most of this, but we've actually got so many folks who came in ahead of time and have been buying things that they keep getting pulled away to help customers." She smiled again. "I have a great team and frankly I'd rather have them serving customers than moving chairs around any day, so if you really don't mind helping that would be super."

She waved her arm at the sea of chairs in front of them. "We got them all out of the storeroom and the tables all put away, so really it's just a matter of straightening them out so it looks comfortable rather than chaotic." She smiled and showed Allison a picture she'd taken at the last special event she had. "This layout worked really well. See how the rows just curve around slightly? It actually gives everyone a little more elbow-room and looks good too."

Allison nodded and the two women set about the task of creating order out of the mess. The work flowed smoothly and soon the last chair was in place.

"Let's sit down here and enjoy a moment's peace before the crowd arrives," Marjorie suggested, waving at the lone "bar table" they'd left in the corner of the cafe.

"How's everything going in *your* world?" Marjorie asked the younger woman. "If I recall, the last time we talked you were experiencing some interesting things as you worked a bit with practicing *acceptance.* Any more happening for you on that front?"

"Well, I'm still working my way through the book and I can't say that I'm *fully* on-board yet, but it actually is starting to make more sense to me and feel more comfortable as a way to approach things. You may remember that when you first told me about that book, I didn't at all like the idea of acceptance, at least not when it came to conditions in my life that I don't want.

"But what I'm getting better at understanding is that accepting my current *state of being* really is different than accepting those unwanted conditions. And that by accepting my current state of being I'm letting go of the resistance that I was feeling and I'm actually becoming open to experiencing the state of being that I really want."

She laughed and shook her head. "I'm not sure I'm explaining that all that well, but at least it is starting to make sense to me."

Marjorie smiled warmly. "I think that was a very

good explanation." She looked over at her makeshift theater. "Oh, and look, people are starting to gather—I should probably excuse myself and go greet them." She looked Allison in the eye and said, "I truly look forward to hearing more about your experiences. Maybe you'll come around some day for lunch in the café and we can chat more."

Marjorie threaded her way through the carefully arranged spread of chairs and was pleased to see that Martin has arrived. She'd made a point of mentioning it to him and encouraging him to come, both because she thought the subject matter would be of real interest to him and also just because she hoped to see him there.

After seeing him into a good seat, she looked up to see Dianne and Chris coming down the center aisle to say hello before sitting down. Dianne, too, was someone she felt might really get a lot out of the movie. She'd gotten an interesting *feeling* from Dianne those few days when she'd come into Lagniappe for her morning coffee. It seemed that even though she wasn't yet ready to admit it, she just might be opening up to a life change.

Marjorie moved gracefully through the room— greeting people, encouraging them to find good seats and settle in—and enjoying the satisfied feeling as she took in the happy buzz of the crowd. She realized they would likely fill just about all the seats and was pleased.

She knew there might be a few stragglers, but it was a few minutes past the start-time for the event and she believed in delivering to people what she'd promised—in this case, an event that began at the stated hour. She made her way to the front of the crowd and greeted the group warmly.

"Welcome and thank you so much for coming out tonight. I know many of you have probably read the book, *HomeGrown*, which was the foundation for this film. For those of you who haven't, let me give you just a quick glimpse into what you'll be seeing.

"The authors have done, in my opinion, a truly wonderful job of looking at something we've all just about taken for granted—the globalization of practically everything in our lives—and encouraged us to consider another way of thinking. A way that brings the focus back into our local communities, a way of life that's more home-grown, from the food we eat to the businesses we support, our relationships with our neighbors and families, and so on.

"It's about recreating our lives to be *sustainable*, for the environment, for our wallets, and dare we say for our souls. I hope you'll enjoy it."

At that she stepped aside, dimmed the lights for better viewing, and turned on the projector. As the screen lit up with the crisp colorful images, she was again grateful that she'd invested last year in the new theater projection system.

She had wondered at the time if it was overkill and a foolish expenditure, but when she held one of these events she felt it was important that the quality be outstanding so that people could really enjoy themselves and get caught up in the movie and not be straining to see much-smaller TV screens. And having her own equipment permanently installed, calibrated, and ready to go rather than renting equipment had proven to be worthwhile. It made putting on an event like this easy, which meant she did it more often.

She smiled with the satisfaction that, as usual, she'd made a good business decision. So much of that came from her consistent use of the principles that had become such an integral part of her life.

Whenever she was worrying over a decision, she found that getting clear on what she *really* wanted, what her *state of being* would be when she had that, then accepting both her current *temporary* state of being of worry and being open to making the right decisions that would allow her to experience her *desired* state of being...well, it just worked for her, over and over again.

Marjorie sat down and quickly became engrossed in the film, just as all her guests did. Out of the corner of her eye she saw her young next-door neighbor and his wife slip into some of the last empty seats at the back. *Good*, she thought, *I'm so glad they came.*

The response of the audience was enthusiastic and sincere as Marjorie turned up the lights again and turned off the projection system. She again spoke to the group.

"I'm delighted to see that you all seem to have enjoyed the film and I thank you for coming. I think we can all agree that there were surely some ideas there that will give us things to think about. Please be sure in the coming days to go to our website at lagniappebookshop.com where you'll be able to hold a virtual conversation with others who have read the book or seen this film. It's a great place to share your own thoughts and ideas and maybe get some good ones from others.

"We have some simple refreshment back at the café counter—a taste of wine for those that like and our secret-recipe iced tea and lemonade. Please feel free to stick around for a bit and chat with your fellow movie-goers."

As people began to get up and mill around, her staff quietly swooped in and removed some of the chairs so there was more room to move about.

Jason came back to find the lights up and people moving around, gathering their things to leave, many staying around for what seemed to be some kind of drinks and snacks back at the café counter. "What's going on?" he asked Roxanne. He'd had to slip out to the restroom just as the ending credits were playing in the film.

"They've got wine and iced tea in back if you want to stay for a bit," she replied. "And a page on their website where comments can be made."

"Oh look!" Jason grabbed Roxanne's arm. There's Martin, the owner of that farm I've been telling you about."

He hurried Rox over to where Martin was standing, concerned that he might leave before he saw Jason and pleased to have this casual opportunity to touch base further about the job possibility Martin had mentioned.

"Martin! Great to see you here," Jason exclaimed, genuinely. "Meet my wife, Roxanne."

The two shook hands and Jason continued, enthusiastically. "We've been talking about the job you mentioned, and I think it could just be a great fit. I'd really like to come to the office soon and talk with you about it more?"

"That sounds great!" Martin replied. "I've got to be away much of tomorrow, but how about you come out the next day, maybe around 10 in the morning? That would give me time to get the morning stuff out of the way first."

"Sounds good to me. Looking forward to it," Jason responded. "How'd you like the film?"

They talked about the movie and the book, which Martin had just finished reading, and found that it had struck the same chords in all three of them. Even Roxanne, who by her own admission didn't really consider that "her thing" the way Martin and Jason did, acknowledged that she'd found a lot of what was shown to be compelling.

Jason and Rox said their goodbyes to Martin, rushing just a bit to get home since Roxanne had a very early shift in the morning. Smithson's didn't normally serve breakfast, but they did occasionally host business meetings and tomorrow she had to be at work at 5 am. It felt like it was already past her bedtime even though the sun hadn't quite left the summer sky.

"You've been really quiet since we left Lagniappe. What did you think of the movie?" Chris asked Dianne as they pulled into their driveway.

There was a thoughtful pause before Dianne replied. "I really liked it, although it made me a little uncomfortable as I look at my own life. I know I don't normally think about most of the things they brought up."

She hesitated again as Chris parked the car and they both got out. "You may think I'm crazy, but there's the beginning of an idea bubbling around in my head." She shook her head slightly, as though that might banish the crazy idea.

"You game to sit up for a bit and talk?" she asked. "Here's what I'm thinking. You know how they talked about investing locally? I know they meant your time and your energy, but also potentially your money."

She paused again and took a deep breath.

"I'm wondering if there might not be some value to my doing some kind of micro-loan program, right here in our own community. It seems whenever we hear about micro-loans they're off in some exotic third world country and I have no doubt those programs are useful. But this movie really made me think about the needs right here at home. We've been through some tough years. I'll bet there's lots of little businesses and projects that need help right here, right now."

She rushed on, afraid to look at Chris. "I have— *we* have—a lot of money saved up. I wonder if some of it might be more usefully invested right here at home."

Her voice trailed off, as if realizing how crazy this must sound. But when she looked up, Chris was looking back at her with clear astonishment and, she was surprised to see, admiration.

Chris smiled gently. "Well, I think that is, indeed, something worthy of sitting up for a bit and talking about."

—Chapter 10

Allison parked her minivan at Lagniappe and hurried in to the café. She'd gotten stuck at the office working with clients through her usual lunchtime and now that it was after two o'clock she was starved.

She ordered the salad and crabcake again with the house-special iced tea and settled in at her table. She'd tucked her copy of *The Power of Acceptance* into her purse and pulled it out to read. She wasn't entirely sure about the etiquette of bringing your own book to a bookstore, but decided that since she'd bought it there in the first place, that must be okay. She opened to the page she'd bookmarked last night when she was reading and picked up where she'd left off.

"Our conditioning says that we can't experience the state of being unless we actually experience the physical thing. Guess what state of being we are experiencing when you we say we need something in order to have something? NEED. Bottom line, the state of being of need creates more opportunities to need.

"I'll bet you can relate to the frustration we've all experienced in the past because we were unaware that we were doing this backwards. We'd say, 'I'll be happy

when....' *What we were actually saying was, 'I need ... in order to experience happiness right now.' So we just kept creating more need and never a true experience of happiness."*

Allison stopped reading as she sensed a presence near her. She looked up to see Marjorie standing right beside her table.

"Sorry—I just wanted to say hello but you seemed so engrossed I didn't want to disturb you. Nice to see you again. And thanks again for your help last night. How'd you like the film?"

"I really enjoyed it. Now I'd like to read the book. That is, if I ever finish this one." She smiled a little ruefully and waved *The Power of Acceptance* at Marjorie. I know it's a short book, but I seem to have to keep re-reading to be sure I'm understanding it. It's actually written perfectly clearly, I guess the problem is with me and not with the book."

Marjorie nodded sympathetically. "It's so true, we humans certainly are plenty capable of getting in our own way, aren't we? Is there any particular area you're struggling with? When we talked last night it sounded like you were really getting it pretty well."

Allison sighed. "Well, you know how I've told you some of what's going on at work. I just feel like by this point in my life it shouldn't be this hard. Rick and I are both good at our work, why are we still struggling so financially?

"I'm the best salesperson at my company, and sales is supposed to pay well, isn't it? But they just don't seem to appreciate me or, at least, they sure aren't showing that appreciation with in my paycheck. I know the economy has been rough, but, hell, this morning I just found about a huge amount the company spent on something else so I just can't believe it's a case of genuinely not being able to afford to pay me more. It just feels like they don't value what I'm doing enough to make it worth more to them.

"I hate the idea of looking for a job somewhere else or even changing fields completely. I know forty-four isn't old or anything, but still I don't really want to be starting over at this point. Plus I couldn't afford to do that even if I did want to. But I just feel so stuck."

She stabbed a piece of crabcake with her fork and ate it while Marjorie patiently sat and waited.

"As I'm reading this book, part of me feels like I really *get it* and part of me thinks I never will. I was just re-reading about the exercise to identify the state of being you'd have if you had the thing you *think* you want, and then drop the *need* for the thing you think you want and acknowledge that *just maybe* it would be possible to have the state of being you want without the thing."

She looked quizzically at Marjorie. "I understand

intellectually the idea that feeling a *need* is putting me in a state of *resistance* and that accepting the possibility of not having the thing I want would be more opening, without so much resistance, but it seems very hard to not want the thing I want."

Marjorie smiled. "Maybe it would help if you didn't think of it so much as not wanting the thing you want, but rather looking *beyond* that *thing* itself to get to the root of what *state of being* it is that you really want to experience.

"When you are willing to *consider* not having something, when you drop the *need* for that thing, that's when you so often actually *get* the very thing it was that you wanted. Just that *willingness to consider* has a remarkable power to open you up and allow in what you want. When you aren't in the state of need, when you've opened up to possibility, that means you've dropped the resistance, and good things happen."

"So by not needing the thing I want, then I can have it?" Allison asked. "It feels like I'm somehow trying to trick the universe into giving me what I want. That can't be how it works."

"Well, that's why this very *simple* practice is not always so *easy*. Yes, the result comes after you drop the need, the resistance, but dropping that need has to be *real*. I think you've probably read the chapter about becoming aware of your state of being, identifying what you're experiencing, and *accepting* it as a tool to help you *get real* about dropping the need.

"Because the way you drop the need is *to accept that you are experiencing need.* Each time you accept your current state of being, a little piece of resistance falls away and you're more aligned with what you really want. It's that *alignment* that allows you to manifest what it is that you desire.

"It's important, too—just as you were describing to me last night—to make the distinction between accepting your *state of being*—which is essential to becoming a conscious creator—and accepting your *current circumstances.* You, for instance, have current circumstances around your job, your income, that you are really struggling with. No one is suggesting that you need to accept those circumstances. What you might try to really play around with more, though, is becoming aware of your state of being about your circumstance, and accepting that. That's where the resistance is."

Allison looked skeptical. "So it would help if I accepted that I'm experiencing frustration? And anger? And being un-appreciated?"

Marjorie nodded. "Yes, although again it's key to make that distinction between circumstances and state of being. As long as you're resisting the state of being— let's say, the experience of frustration—you're creating more and more opportunity to experience it, because that's what you're aligned with, that's your 'vibration' if you will. Ironically, once you can say to yourself, 'I accept that I'm experiencing frustration right now and that's okay,' then your vibration changes."

She looked Allison in the eye. "It's not my place to tell you what you're feeling or how to act. But based on what you've told me, it seems that the thing you think you want is to be appropriately compensated at work and not to be struggling financially. And if you had that, then you'd feel appreciated and valued and even relaxed since you wouldn't be worrying about money. So you might look at those as the states of being that you want, right? In your current frustration and anger, you think that you *need* a different job—or certainly different circumstances at your current job— to experience those things.

"So, there you are, back to the issue with *need*, right? And that puts you back to playing around more with the idea that you're *willing to consider* that you don't need that actual thing—a different job—in order to experience those states of being. It's funny, but just that willingness creates a huge release in the resistance, in the need. And without the resistance, things start to open up.

"But, you know, you can only read about it and talk about it so much. Basically, you just have to do it."

Allison nodded. "I know. I've always been prone to feel like I need to understand it all just perfectly before I can do anything. Do you remember the when we had lunch a while back, after I was first reading the book and you wrote out something for me. It included the line, "I'm willing to consider the possibility that I don't need to understand in order to experience comfort, control, and power right now."

She shook her head and then smiled wryly. "That seems like the line I most need to work with. But I think I get it when you say that just acknowledging that I could 'consider' something has a power. I think I always want it to be so black and white, but that feels like an in-between that I could live with. And, to tell the truth, as I was telling you last night, whenever I do remember to practice that, somehow things do have a way of working out better. That's what you mean when you say it helps me drop the resistance, the need, right?"

Marjorie nodded. "Yes, I agree, I think you *are* getting it. Am I remembering that that process that you were just describing continued on with helping you identify whatever *limiting beliefs* you might have about that particular issue? That's some really helpful stuff to work with, too."

Allison looked open to hearing more, so Marjorie described her own "mid-life crisis" fifteen years before when she had worked at Maxwell Pharmaceutical. She told how her she spent years not even recognizing how frustrated she was.

"Once I read this book," she said, nodding toward Allison's copy, "I discovered that I had this *huge* limiting belief. I really believed that was the best I was entitled to. I was smart, I knew that from my school days and from doing the job, but I was overweight, I'd failed at my marriage, I'd never worked anywhere else, my parents had taught me that it was important to 'stick it out' even though nothing seemed to have worked out. It seemed that being unhappy in that job was what I deserved."

She shook her head. "It was crazy, really, but for a long time it simply felt very real to me. That book helped me realize that I didn't want to believe that, and that I had the power to create a new belief. And using that 'I am willing to consider' language was a key.

"For me, that job really was the wrong one and leaving it was the right thing. But you can't make those decisions—at least not make them well—until you can drop the need, drop the limiting belief, and be willing to consider. Because maybe that job you've had for a long time, that you say you're really good at, is absolutely the right job for you, if you started to experience it differently."

Now Allison looked puzzled. "If I experienced it differently? What do you mean?"

"Well, it's all kind-of connected to the 'willing to consider' idea. What if you were willing to consider that you might experience satisfaction, appreciation, and more financial freedom now, without necessarily changing jobs. And what if you spent time accepting your current state of being, as it came up, while also being willing to consider a better state of being.

"And what if you started looking around your job and your life for things to appreciate. Even just the little things. In my own life, at least, I've found that when I start looking for things to appreciate, I find a lot of them, things I never would have even noticed if I weren't looking. Somehow that, too, seems to really ramp up my state of being since when I'm aligned with appreciating things, it seems I get more good stuff to appreciate.

"There's no way to know for sure until you do it, but I have my suspicions that you might find that things improved for you—whether in that job itself, or because a better opportunity presented itself."

She stood up and moved to clear away Allison's dishes, knowing that Allison not only needed to get back to work, but had probably heard enough to make her head swim just a little. "After all, what do you really have to lose?"

Allison glanced at her watch as she settled into

bed with her book. It was late, she really should get right to sleep. But she wanted to at least finish that one section she had been reading at lunch.

She'd just closed the book when Marjorie joined her without putting her bookmark in place, so she had to thumb through the pages for a few moments to find her place. Ah ha, there it was. *"That is why we want to make a conscious effort to drop the need, and it's so easy. Simply say, 'I am willing to consider that I don't need (the end result you want) in order to experience (the states of being that will create the end result) right now.*

Allison put the bookmark carefully in place and set the book on her bedside table, remembering what Marjorie had suggested. *How had she said it? Seems like it was something like this, "I am willing to consider that I don't need to change jobs in order to experience more satisfaction and financial freedom." I'll have to think about that.*

It was her last conscious thought as she drifted off to sleep. *"I am willing to consider...."*

—Chapter 11

Marjorie looked contentedly around Lagniappe, chairs arranged neatly, a raised platform in front with two comfortable armchairs. The authors of one of her very favorite books, *The Power of Acceptance*, were coming this evening to talk about the principles and practices in the book and to introduce their new book, to be published soon.

The Power of Acceptance had meant so much to her over the years, and she'd shared it with so many other people—she felt a little star-struck, knowing that the authors would be right in her little shop soon. As she knew to do, she accepted that she was experiencing nervousness and that was okay. She relaxed almost immediately.

She felt a warm hand on her shoulder and turned around, delighted to see the hand was attached to her friend, Martin. He greeted her with a kiss and then said, "Let me introduce you to my new associate and your caterer for this evening."

Jason had been looking down, watching his step as he walked through the shop carrying a crate of food, and shifted the box into his left arm so that he could shake Marjorie's hand. Surprise lit up his face as he realized he was shaking hands with his next-door neighbor.

"*You're* Marjorie?" He shook his head in disbelief. "That's too much! Martin's been talking about you for weeks but I just never made the connection. In fact, I'm really embarrassed now to realize that I never knew your name or that you owned Lagniappe."

Martin looked puzzled so Marjorie smiled and explained. "This is my next-door neighbor, who is apparently the very same Jason that you've been telling *me* about for weeks. We've chatted many a time over the fence, so to speak, and I've also many a time thought I needed to ask his name, but as you can see, we both somehow managed to skip that step."

Jason added, "You know how it is when you've talked with someone a bunch of times, it starts to feel awkward to say 'oh, by the way, what's your name?' so I guess neither of us did. That's so funny."

Marjorie nodded in agreement. "I haven't seen you around much lately, and now I can see why. It seems you've been busy, at least from what Martin's told me."

Jason set down his crate on the café counter and turned to Marjorie, still shaking his head slightly in surprise. "I've been really busy and in such a great way!" he told her enthusiastically.

"First, as it sounds like you know, I started working part-time with Martin. I suppose you could say I'm just a salesman, but I love it. I go to restaurants and chefs and caterers and show them what the VanElton Farm can offer them, and help them understand why buying even just *some* of their stuff locally can be great for their business and the community."

Marjorie smiled. "Well, in some ways I'm *just a salesman*, too—I sell books and sandwiches to people. I think 'sales' sometimes gets a bad rap. After all, when you've got a great product or a great message—or, ideally, both—and you share that with people in a genuine way that shows your excitement for your product and then give them the space to decide whether or not they want to buy what you're selling...well, I think that's just about one of the finest jobs around!"

Jason looked slightly embarrassed. "Sure, I didn't mean there was anything wrong with being a salesman. It's just that it feels like so much more to me, like I'm really helping to educate folks, giving them the knowledge to see why even small changes they make can make big differences over time."

Marjorie smiled again, both at Jason and then over at Martin. "Yes, I'd say that's important work to be doing, and clearly a job you love, so sounds like a winner to me. But you said that was 'first', so are there other things you're doing now, too?"

Martin interjected briefly to say he'd go out to Jason's truck and get the rest of the food. Jason noticed how Marjorie's eyes followed him as he walked away. *Definitely something there*, he thought. He knew from all that Martin had said about Marjorie over the past weeks that *he* really felt something special for *her*.

Marjorie turned back to Jason and he wondered briefly about how much to tell her. As always, though, her open face looked sincerely interested and he just somehow felt like she would *get* it. "Well, it's interesting that the authors of *The Power of Acceptance* are here tonight, because in some strange way, I feel like that book is all intertwined with the *other* stuff that's been happening for me.

"I don't know if you remember that I did this catering job this past summer? Well, technically it was a private chef job—I had to do all the cooking at the client's house—and that client was Dianne Sanchez. Now that I know that *you* are *you*, I realize you must know her too."

Marjorie nodded, curious to hear how Jason was going to tie all this together.

"I'm not exactly sure what order all this happened in, but somehow she got turned onto that book—I guess probably you were the one who did that—and I saw a copy at her house when I did her dinner party. Totally did *not* seem like it would be my thing—or even *her* thing, from what little I knew about her—but something about it caught my eye. Then when I went to work with Martin I saw that he had a copy, too, which he lent to me after I asked about it.

"Meanwhile—like I say, when I think back I'm not entirely clear on the timetable—Dianne starts this micro-loan program and I end up getting a loan from her to start my business for real. With people I met doing the work with Martin, I've been able to rent time as I need it in licensed commercial kitchens so that I'm not limited to just the private chef part, I can do true off-site catering as well, like this."

Marjorie nodded encouragingly. She suspected it was easier for him to talk about the basic facts of his business rather than what he might see as the more mystical benefits of *The Power of Acceptance.*

"Anyway, as I said, Martin lent me his copy of that book and even though it seemed a little *woo-woo* to me, it also just really *spoke* to me somehow. I made a ton of notes as I was reading so I could give him back his book and remember what it said.

"Then, I just started accepting. That is, I guess I stopped fighting my circumstances, stopped blaming them for how I felt, and just accepted stuff as it came up, acknowledging that whatever state of being I was experiencing was okay. Also learning to allow in the potential to feel good, and what do you know, good stuff started happening!"

Marjorie nodded again. She was well familiar with the experience, but it still thrilled her a little each time she saw someone new come to understand it. "Yes, it's pretty amazing what can happen if we can just stop resisting and start accepting. The challenge so many people seem to have is that—at least at first—it just seems like the opposite of what you want to do. It seems hard to accept the very thing you don't want.

"When I first discovered the book, years ago, it felt like that book and the techniques it described really helped me see the difference between accepting the 'outcome' I didn't want and accepting the sensation, the state of being, I was *experiencing* about that outcome— the sensation of fear or frustration or unworthiness or anger...whatever it was. As soon as I learned to accept— or stop resisting—my state of being, then it was remarkable how things would open up, sometimes almost magically it seemed."

Now it was Jason's turn to nod enthusiastically. "That's exactly it! When I was first laid off from my job, I'd read a little bit about the power of our thoughts and how they affect things. But when I just tried to resist the negative thoughts—like being angry and frustrated—and lay happy, positive thoughts on top of them, that didn't seem to work at all and just felt fake. I guess that works for some people, but it sure didn't seem to be helping me, so I stopped even trying that.

"But, like you say, that book really helped me see the difference between, say, just wallowing in being pissed off—which I think I'd done plenty of!—and really accepting what I was experiencing, without judging it. In fact, the part of the process where you say 'and that's okay' turned out to be very powerful for me. Once I stopped resisting, it's like I suddenly didn't have bad things I needed to resist. And…now, here I am." He grinned.

"In fact, I'm glad I saw you here since I won't see you at home much anymore. Rox and I are moving out next week into our own place."

"That's great news!" Marjorie exclaimed. I know Walt and Louise will miss having you there with them, but I'm sure you're ready to be back on your own, too. That's wonderful." She smiled at him sincerely.

"It's really good to see you and hear how things are going for you. I'd better get out there and talk with some of the other guests, and I suspect you have work to do here so I'll leave you to it. Martin tells me your food is superb, so I'm looking forward to the reception after their talk." She caught sight of Chris and Dianne across the room and waved at them.

Marjorie started across the room and within a few steps they met up and greeted each other warmly.

Martin arrived with the last box of food for the

reception and watched Marjorie as she walked away. He set the crate down and looked at Jason quizzically. "I have to say that's a bit bizarre that *my* Marjorie is *your* next door neighbor." He shook his head. "But, I guess the even more interesting thing is that she probably wouldn't even be *my* Marjorie if it hadn't been for that book."

Martin continued to help Jason unpack the food crate, but moving slowly as he was clearly thinking back over the past months, and even the past years before that.

"I don't know if I've ever told you that before Marjorie introduced me to *The Power of Acceptance*, I was just totally stuck. Stuck in the past. Stuck in my grief. Stuck in believing that somehow I'd been cheated in my life where I'd followed this spiritual path that had turned on me and stolen my wife from me.

"Even as I say that now it sounds melodramatic and maybe even just silly, but it didn't feel silly at the time. It felt like the only real thing in my life. A black, dark thing, but still the only real thing. But meeting Marjorie and then reading—and really working with— that book... well, that changed everything. It was like it made all the spiritual seeking I'd been doing in my life up until then make sense, at least as far as where I'd gone astray.

"And once I started accepting and going through

the exercises about considering the possibility of, well, whatever, it was like light came into my life and my grief just broke open. It had gone beyond real grief anyway, it was more of a strangling sense of the great unfairness of it all."

Martin shook his head, looking embarrassed. "I haven't actually said any of that out-loud, not even to Marjorie." He looked at Jason, who was looking back at him with full empathy. "But it seems like you, of all people, might really understand."

Jason nodded and touched the older man lightly on the arm. "Although the *cause* was different—my loss was just my career to your much-harder loss of your wife—"

Martin interrupted him. "But that was what I came to see; it was really about much more than losing Lynn, it was like I'd lost faith, in anything but mostly in myself."

Jason nodded again. "Yes, I understand. I was so angry about losing my job and not being able to find another, I had the same feeling of losing faith in myself, in my ability, in my basic worth. I wanted something outside of me to fix it. I'd be okay once I got a job, once we didn't have to live at Rox's parents, once I was again valued.

"You might even remember when I first came to work with you that I had these terrible headaches? I assumed they were caused by stress—although I kept putting off going to the doctor, and there was always this nagging sense that it might be something serious. But, anyway, they didn't just magically go away when I got the job with you and the stress lessened.

"I almost hate to even say it since it sounds a little crazy, but they only went away when I borrowed the book from you and started first accepting the experience and then being willing to consider that I could just be pain-free, that I didn't need anything *outside* of my life to cure the headache."

He shook his head and laughed. "I haven't had a headache now in...well, forever it seems."

Martin nodded. "No, I don't think you're crazy. I think this stuff is very powerful, especially learning that technique about being willing to consider something. That was really a key to my turning the business around, too.

"I mean, we'd done okay. My family had worked the farm for a long time and made a living at it, but sometimes only just. When I seriously stopped to look at it, and at myself, I found that I was really struggling with the conflict—or, what felt like a conflict to me, at least—between my spirituality, which I considered to be an integral and vital part of who I am, and the whole experience of making money. You know, good money, wealth even. Somehow the two didn't seem to mesh.

"But once I started accepting that and once I started being willing to consider that there was no conflict, that I could run my business in a way that could be really profitable, not just scraping by, that's when things opened up for me."

The two men looked over to where Marjorie was talking with Dianne and Chris in time to see Marjorie motioning back toward them. Although they couldn't hear, they wouldn't have been surprised that she was saying to Dianne, "It sure looks like your microloan program is working! At least there's one satisfied client there."

Dianne smiled broadly back at her. "I know, it sure feels great to be able to use our money for things that can do a lot of good right here at home. That's a bright young man and he's going to go far. He just needed a little bit of help to get him going.

"In fact, you might get a kick out of this—you know he catered a dinner party for me a while back. Well, it sounds really odd to say but I ended up not really knowing his full name.

"He went by *Jay*, at least on his nametag the day I met him, and that's all I'd ever called him. I paid him cash so I never got his name for writing a check or anything. His email was just 'chef@some-domain-I-don't-remember-dot-com' so when I got the application from Jason Coulter, I actually didn't realize that was *him.* It wasn't until we met for his initial funding interview that I was able to put it all together!"

Marjorie laughed with her. "Well, I'm just delighted that it all worked out. What a transformation from the bitter, discouraged person he had become to the cheerful and *productive* fellow we see there now. He'd worked really hard to develop his skills, but he just needed that little bit of breathing room with your micro-loan."

Dianne nodded. "And you know it's such a win-win. These recipients of the loans work really hard to pay them back, I can charge them a very fair interest and still be making more on my money than many other investments these days, and they're getting funds at a good interest rate that they couldn't even *get* otherwise. I'm so glad I did this! Thanks largely to *you* and your showing of that *HomeGrown* film—that's where I got the idea."

Dianne shook her head slightly and continued. "Actually, I should be more accurate. The specific idea for the micro-loan program came from that, but truthfully the *much* more important contribution you made was getting me to buy that book *The Power of Acceptance* from you!

"It was a little while before I got around to reading it—I'll confess I think I bought it just because that was easier than explaining to you that I wasn't interested. It did not *at all* seem like a subject I *would* really be interested in, but once I started the book I could hardly put it down. It felt like it was talking directly to me, telling me just what I needed to hear.

"I started practicing the exercises in the book, learning how to 'accept' and also being 'willing to consider' and things just busted wide open for me—in a good way!"

Chris had been listening attentively to Dianne and now joined in. "Did Dianne tell you her other big news?"

Marjorie shook her head in reply, asking, "What? What's the news?"

Dianne laughed and nodded to Chris, saying, "You tell." She looked back to Marjorie with the explanation, "Chris always enjoys telling folks since it's been such a good change for us."

"Dianne left Maxwell finally!" Chris reported triumphantly. "She's now working as VP of Marketing for Integrative Health. You know, that chain of wellness centers that recently moved their headquarters here."

At that Dianne broke back in. "Yes, Chris finally got through to me that Maxwell really wasn't about creating health but about treating symptoms—often symptoms caused by the very drugs Maxwell had sold someone to treat some other symptom!—and once I fully *got* the difference, the job just wasn't the same.

It's really exciting for me to apply my years of business experience to a company that I *do* really believe it."

She smiled wryly. "Of course, it has meant giving up a few of the things we'd gotten used to—it's a smaller company without the astronomical profits you see in the pharmaceutical world, but it has been so worth it."

Marjorie smiled at them both. "Well, I must say, you look great, so the job change seems to suit you. In fact, speaking of suits, I think this might be the first time I've ever seen you not wearing one."

Dianne nodded. "You know, it's ironic—Chris has always worn pants, but she always has these great scarves and flow-y tops, and everything seems so soft. I've loved her clothes but never felt I could dress like that. I've always worn a skirt, but as part of a very tailored business suit and in *all* these years it never really felt like me, but it just felt necessary. Now I can dress the way I feel and for once I can even borrow some of Chris's clothes!" She laughed, "which is a good thing since I feel like I'm starting a wardrobe from scratch again."

She went on to say, "But wait. Chris told you about *my* big news, but not about her own. You know that empty shop two doors down from you? She's about to close a deal to rent it. She's planning on opening a 'wellness shop' of sorts with natural products, essential oils, some organic food, a treatment room for massage and such. Still lots of details to iron out but it looks good."

Chris was nodding happily while Dianne told Marjorie her plans and her smile widened when Marjorie said, "Oh, you've *got to* meet my friend, Martin. He owns VanElton farms and they have wonderful locally grown, organic foods. He also sells some other things from nearby farms, like the *best* bison! He's been talking about trying to get into some retail outlets, so it's a perfect match! Oh, excellent, here he comes now."

Marjorie saw Martin walking toward them and waved him over. Putting her hand on his arm, she smiled happily. "Martin, I want you to meet some old friends of mine. This is Dianne Sanchez, a co-worker of mine from a former lifetime, and her wife, Chris. They've got some interesting things going on and I know you'd enjoy talking. Specifically, too, Chris is looking into opening a shop just down the way here, and carrying natural foods. Seems like a match made in heaven, if you'll pardon the trite expression."

As Chris and Martin talked enthusiastically about the potentials of doing business together, Marjorie walked a few steps away where she stopped to talk with Allison.

"Oh, am I glad to see you!" Allison exclaimed, reaching out to spontaneously hug Marjorie. "I'm sorry

—it feels like forever since I've been in to see you. I've just been *so* busy at work. And at home for that matter, we're *finally* doing some remodeling we've really needed to do."

Marjorie looked pleased, guessing that Allison might have finally "gotten" the concepts of *The Power of Acceptance* she'd been struggling with, so she asked, "Do tell? Last time we'd talked you were still really struggling with the job, with tight finances, lots of frustration.... Sounds like maybe things got better?"

Allison laughed lightly. "I can hardly believe how much things got better. And I really have you to thank for turning me on to *The Power of Acceptance*. I know when we last met I felt like I was wrestling with some of it, but I actually finally took to heart the book's recommendation to *accept* that I was experiencing struggle and resistance, and as I did that I also really starting working with the idea of *being willing to consider* that I didn't have to have my job change in order to be fulfilled, have more money, and so on. At first it seemed awkward, but before long it started to seem more natural, but even more importantly, things actually started to change."

Marjorie nodded. *Yep, things do start to change.* "Tell me more," she encouraged Allison.

"Well, you may remember that I just felt *so* frustrated, like I was totally not being appreciated, certainly the appreciation wasn't reflected in my salary. I was so flippin' tired of the constant financial struggle and, maybe even worse was just the sense that I wasn't being valued.

"So at first being willing to consider that I didn't need things to change at work seemed crazy—I mean, how would anything in my life change if it didn't change at work?—but I just kept accepting and being willing to consider and the damnedest thing happened.

"The Wosniak brothers who own the business just seemed to wake up one day and see me for the first time. First they just started noticing and actually complimenting me on my work with our clients. And then they offered me what's essentially a whole new position in the company.

"I'm still designing and selling houses, but I've also implemented a training program for the other design consultants which I love doing. And they gave me a true management position, with some real profit sharing so I'm making so much more money. And with my training program, the whole business is doing well, so everyone's happy."

She shook her head. "As you know, I sure didn't grab on to the *The Power of Acceptance* principles all that easily, but I sure don't think I'd be where I am now, no way, without that book and doing the work. I really want to thank you."

Marjorie smiled and nodded up to the platform where Doreen and Arden were sitting, chatting with each other, getting ready to begin their talk. "Maybe you'll get a chance to thank *them*. I'm just the means of getting the book into your hands, they're the ones who wrote it!"

Allison nodded. "I'm really glad that you've brought them here. I'm looking forward to hearing them speak, and the book has meant so much to me, it's exciting to see them."

As Allison was settling in to her seat, Marjorie started toward the front of the room to introduce her special guests. She backed up a step, though, and asked Allison, "How's Rick?"

Allison smiled broadly. "He's great. He wanted to come tonight but he's got a big project going on and he wants to be sure it will come in on schedule, so he's been working a lot lately. But he loves the work and is happy to be so busy.

"He hasn't yet gotten around to reading *The Power of Acceptance* but we've talked about it some and he's sure been interested to see what's been going on for me. I thought I'd buy him his own copy tonight and have it signed for him as a gift. I'm sure that whenever the time is right, he'll enjoy reading it."

Marjorie smiled her agreement and went forward again to introduce her guests. She spoke from her heart to the gathered crowd about how *The Power of Acceptance* had changed her own life and how pleased she was to have the authors in her little shop, then stepped off the platform, turning the presentation over to them.

Doreen spoke first, telling how she had come to do this work, leaving the corporate world behind to become a life coach, then getting a book contract for *Excuse Me, Your Life is Now* as a follow-up to the hugely popular *Excuse Me, Your Life is Waiting* by Lynn Grabhorn.

She explained, "I touched on 'acceptance' in *Your Life is Now*. I'd written then that 'when you accept what doesn't feel good, you release that energy and can use it to keep your thoughts and feelings on the positive results that you really want.' But that hadn't been a focus of Lynn's work, and it really wasn't a focus of *Your Life is Now*.

"But as my work with clients over the years continued, I continued to see that that's where so many folks were struggling. They'd heard so much about positive thinking that they felt like they were doing something wrong if they accepted their fears, jealousies, anxieties, frustrations, and limiting beliefs." She looked out over the room to see lots of heads nodding in agreement.

"I began to emphasize more with clients this

need for acceptance, the necessity of releasing resistance. I found that if I could even just get them to be being *willing to consider* that they could accept, that things would actually change for them.

"Your point of attraction is always your state of being. You are always creating opportunities to expand and experience more of your current state of being. So when you are resisting, your state of being of resistance creates more opportunities to experience resistance, which is another way of saying experience more of what you don't want. Not exactly what most people are trying for!

"Acceptance is the key for changing your *perception* of your current circumstances, which is the only thing that will actually change your circumstances. Even when what you're accepting is that you're experiencing resistance, that still works." She laughed.

"I know, it sometimes seems counterintuitive, but I can simply tell you that I've seen it work over and over again with my clients. And, of course, I've seen it in my own life. When I was first thinking about writing my next book, I realized that when I was really honest with myself, I wanted to work *with* a great writer and not have to write it all myself.

"I can tell you that I spent a good bit of time *accepting*—accepting that I was experiencing confusion, and that that was okay. Accepting that I didn't know where I would find this writer and being willing to consider that the right inspiration would come.

"And it did! I realized I had an email list of hugely talented people, why didn't I start there. The rest, as they say, is history!"

She waved her arm at Arden as she said it. "I got responses from a number of potential collaborators, each of whom offered something interesting, but the sample Arden wrote let me know that she completely *got* my work, *got* what I was hoping to create with the book, and it felt right. So we wrote *The Power of Acceptance* together as a 'cookbook' of sorts. Arden, maybe you'd like to say a bit more about it, and about the new book too?"

Arden nodded at Doreen and smiled out at the crowd. "Thanks. As Doreen said, she sent an email out to her list with a subject line of 'Calling All Writers' and although I got it first thing in the morning, it was much later that day before I replied. It seemed to take me those hours to fully accept the idea that, 'hey, I'm a writer, I know and respect Doreen's material, I should do this!' I wrote back to her that day and over the next several weeks we spoke on the phone, exchanged more emails, and exactly one month later had come to an agreement that we would write this book together.

"We wanted *The Power of Acceptance* to be an easy to read book that would help people understand the need for acceptance in order to allow in the good they wanted. A book with examples and exercises to help someone move beyond the theoretical to the practical. And I'm pleased that that book has helped millions of people.

"And now we've hopefully done it again with this new book. We wanted to help inspire folks by telling the stories of others who'd struggled and experienced success in their lives once they incorporated acceptance into their lives, really learned how to use it as an invaluable tool to help them become the conscious creators they're capable of being. We wanted to show folks who learned to use acceptance to allow in the good that is theirs. We love this book and hope you will too!"

She nodded back to Doreen, who read a couple of passages from the book. As Arden looked out over the sea of faces, she was gratified to see how interested they looked. They seemed to be listening with rapt attention. She noticed the shop owner, Marjorie, was surveying the scene with a look of the same appreciation that Arden felt.

Marjorie listened as Doreen finished reading from the book. Doreen closed the presentation by encouraging everyone to stay for the reception and saying that she and Arden looked forward to talking with them and hearing their stories.

Marjorie looked around the crowded room, her eyes resting briefly on Jason, Martin, Allison, and Dianne. She smiled to herself. *This new book of Doreen's and Arden's will surely help others understand and see the principles in action, but I see all the evidence I could ever want right here in this room.*

Dear readers—As you might well have figured out, **this** *book you've been reading is the real-life combination of* **The Power of Acceptance** *(the book portrayed here as having been written a number of years ago)* **and** *the "new book" that Doreen and Arden are talking about in this last chapter. We hope you'll allow us this bit of artistic license as a way to bring you both the practical "nuts and bolts" explanations and techniques (primarily incorporated into Part Two of this book) along with an engaging story. Perhaps you've seen something of yourself in Allison, Jason, Martin, or Dianne and can now better imagine for yourself how using these powerful tools in your own life might benefit you. Please read on, put into practice what you read, and let us know about your experiences.*

Email us: comments@the-power-of-acceptance.com

Part Two

Doreen Banaszak

Table of Contents

—Chapter 1
Journey Beyond Frustration

What if the power to be, to do, to have, to know anything were inside of me and all I had to do to awaken it was to simply acknowledge it and allow it to give me all I ever wanted?,,,. What if I actually consciously used this power to create my life? What if?...

I, like you, wanted to believe all the "what ifs" and thought I had a pretty good grasp on the whole Law of Attraction process. Heck, I wrote a book about it. What I found frustrating after I wrote the book was that while I created circumstances I wanted to experience (albeit not consistently) I still didn't feel happy and successful after the experience. Crazy, I know, but true! I was still missing something. I was still missing the understanding of what our creative power really is.

When I feel like I am missing something or I think I don't know something, I head right to the bookstore. There my quest is to scan the spines in search of the title that will solve my problem. Once found, I go home, start digging in, and feel as though this book will be the answer to my problem.

Then, three months later, I find the book, with the answer to my problem, unread, covered in dust, next to a pile of books with a little less dust, all meant to solve the very same problem the first book promised to. The Japanese have a word for this phenomenon, Tsundoku—buying books and not reading them; letting books pile up unread on shelves or floors or nightstands. Let's be honest, do you Tsundoku? I know I did!

It seems the more I would seek, the more opportunities I got to seek. I never *found*. This was curious and was a great fulfillment of the definition of insanity according to Einstein—doing the same thing over and over again expecting a different result. Well it was time to get "sane."

If every time I would seek, I got more opportunities to seek then why not endeavor to do the opposite. But the opposite was a little hard to comprehend because the opposite required me to decide that I already knew the answer.

What? How could I know something I knew I didn't know? It didn't make sense to go back to seeking, so I had to bite the bullet and be *willing to consider* that I could know the answer.

So that's what I did. I said...

I'm willing to consider I know exactly what it is that creates.

And, to my surprise, I was successfully able to resist every urge to storm the doors of the bookstore. I was even successful in resisting Googling, "What is our power to create?"

Now the skies didn't open up and angels did not descend and whisper the answer in my ear, but what did happen was, within a few days, I started having new thoughts. Up until this point my thoughts ran along the lines of...

- Why does the Law of Attraction work for my clients but not all the time for me?
- Why can't I get consistent results?
- Why is creating so hard?
- I'm frustrated!
- I'm tired of thinking positively, and trying to "vibrate" at levels I don't even know I can reach.

These thoughts were replaced by several new thoughts, the first of which was...

1. Whatever "it" is that actually creates has to create absolutely.

It didn't make sense that the creative power would create in one area of my life, but not create in another area. It also didn't make sense that this creative power would have a personality or the ability to judge and then not perform for me according to its mood. If it did, I would truly be a powerless victim.

So whatever this creative power is, it has to create absolutely. So what creates absolutely?

There are lots of theories out there on what actually creates. We've been told that thoughts create, that feelings create, that words create, and that actions create.

Well if whatever the creative power is creates absolutely then every thought, feeling, word, and action would have to create, absolutely. I don't know about you, but life would be pretty scary if every thought I had actually manifested, or for that matter every feeling, word, or action. Life would certainly be interesting, but probably not in such a good way.

The only conclusion I could draw from this analysis was that thoughts, feelings, words, and actions can *not* be the creative power.

I have to admit that this was a bit of relief because I was getting very tired of managing all my thoughts, feelings, words, and actions. It was exhausting! On the other hand, in one fell swoop, I just negated a big chunk of what I had learned (and taught) about the Law of Attraction. That was a little scary, but I went with it.

The thought that followed was...

2. Whatever "it" is that creates, I have to be using it right now, therefore "it" has to exist right now.

This made sense because it would be impossible for me to use this power in the past or future, because the only place I can be is here. The only time I can use this power is right now.

So then I looked at thoughts, feelings, words, and actions again. As soon as I have a thought it is in the past, same with a feeling, a word, and an action. I know it seems like thoughts, feelings, words, and actions are ongoing, but what we are really experiencing is a succession of them. They don't exist right now, they move into the past as soon as they are experienced.

So then the question became, "What exists here and now?" The only thing that exists here and now is what I am experiencing here and now. I am always experiencing, but what is it? It's not a thought, feeling, word, or action since I'd already established that they can't exist now because once experienced they are in the past. Then the idea came to me that the only thing I am constantly experiencing is a *state of being.*

Okay...a state of being? I was willing to consider I knew what a state of being was and this is what came up...

States of being are invisible forces inside of us.

These forces range from love to hatred and everything in between. These invisible forces are the creative juice behind all of our experiences. They are actually the cause of our feelings, thoughts, words, actions, and reality.

Now I felt I was just making things up, but aren't we all just making this up as we go? So I stayed with it.

My next realization was—and take note because this is the most important realization in this book—all states of being exist inside of me, right now.

Why is this so amazing? Because, I had been running around saying things like...

- I'll be happy when I'm doing work I love.
- I'll be wealthy when I have plenty of money in the bank.
- I'll be healthy when I lose 20 pounds.
- I'll experience love when I meet my soul mate.

Well, happiness, wealth, health, and love exist inside of me right now so I already have them and don't have to wait for anything to experience them.

You may be saying, "But I do want to be doing work I love, have plenty of money in the bank, lose 20 pounds, and meet my soul mate." Of course, and you can and should, but consider what you *ultimately* want.

Most people, including myself, think we want the "thing"—the money, the car, the house, the soul mate.

But if pressed, we find that there is really something we want much more.

Here is a typical conversation I would have with someone about money...

"So what do you want?"

"I want more money."

"Great! Now what will you experience when you have more money that you aren't experiencing now?"

"I would experience wealth and security."

"Great, now if money didn't give you the state of wealth and security, would you still want it?"

"Sure because I could afford to buy all the things I wanted."

"And what would you experience when you could afford to buy all the things you wanted?"

"Happiness."

"Okay, and if money didn't bring you the state of wealth, security, and happiness, would you still want the money?"

"Yes, because I could pay off all my debt."

"And what would you experience if you paid off all your debt?"

"Relief."

"And if money didn't bring you wealth, security, happiness, and relief would you still want the money?"

"Well, no."

"That's because what you ultimately want is to

experience the states of being you think you will experience when you have the money."

So we already have what we ultimately want, the states of being we want to experience, inside of us right now. Welcome to the "kingdom within." And the best part? The price we have to pay to experience the external things we want is to experience the wonderful states of being we *ultimately* want, *right now*! Can there be anything more amazing to consider?

So if you want to experience a relationship with a soul mate, you simply experience the states of being you think you will experience once you are in that relationship, but you experience them now. So you have to be willing to experience love and joy and beauty and connection right now. What a steep price to pay, huh?

We've had it backwards. We've thought that when we get the physical thing, *then* we'll experience what we ultimately want, the state of being. It's the opposite, when you experience what you ultimately want, the state of being, then that state creates the physical thing you want. Is it any wonder we've been so frustrated?

More on this later, in the meantime, more questions came up...

3. **This is all very exciting, but what is my role in this creative process?**

Supposedly I'm the creator of my reality, but if this is the case, why do I often feel as though I'm the victim of my reality and not the creator? Who am I in this creative process?

For a long time I had been personally identifying with my states of being. For example, I would say things like, "I am angry", or "I am happy." Once I identified with them, then when I was angry I would judge myself because it wasn't okay to be angry. Or, when I identified myself as "being" happy, it became *not okay* when I *wasn't* happy. In addition as soon as I said, "I am angry" (or "I am not happy") I was locked into that state. I couldn't experience anything else.

I realized that I was tying my identity to something I could never be. How do I know I could never *be* anger? Simple, if I *was* anger I would have to be angry all the time, which of course I'm not. So it is easily proven that we are *not* our experience.

What am I then? I am here to experience myself so therefore I must *be the experiencer* who chooses their experience.

That made sense because the one constant in life is that we are always experiencing something. If I am the experiencer, then that must mean that I am in charge of whatever it is that creates my experience.

Well, if states of being are the creative juice responsible for creating everything else, then that must be what I am constantly doing—whether I am aware of it or not—*choosing* a state of being and that state of being is the thing that *manifests* as my feelings, thoughts, words, actions, and my reality. That would mean that...

I am the master of my state of being and my chosen state of being is the master of everything else in my life including my reality.

I like to think of it like this...I am the master of my state of being. I choose a state, let's say happiness. Then that *state of being*—the master of everything else—goes to the body and says, "She chose happiness, give her happy feelings." Then it goes to the brain and says, "She chose happiness, give her happy thoughts. Remind her why in the past she was happy, why she is happy now, and why she is going to be happy in the future."

Truth be told, I was excited by this notion because I was literally exhausted trying to think positively, vibrate my feelings at a high frequency, say only positive things when I didn't really mean them, and act in ways that weren't congruent with how I was feeling.

Now I only have to keep my eye on *one* thing and that one thing would naturally change all that followed, including my experience.

If I'm the experiencer and by default the creator of my reality, then I have to be free to choose *any* state of being because a creator can't be hindered by anything—if they were, then they would be a victim, not a creator.

So I have to be free to choose love or hatred, fear or courage, happiness or frustration. That means all states of being are actually okay, but more on this in a bit.

Could this be true? I am the experiencer, free to choose any state of being and therefore manifest anything I want? I was willing to find out, but first more new thoughts...

So the creative power is my state of being and that state of being is the *cause* of my feelings, thoughts, words, actions, and reality which all can be categorized now as the *effect*.

What happens when you try to change an *effect*? Nothing! It is only when you deal with *cause* that things actually can change. It's like trying to fix a mistake on a document you printed off the computer by erasing the mistake on the paper rather than going back into your file on the computer and making the change there. It might be fixed temporarily on that one page, but the next time you print it, it will still be there. Trying to fix the outcome can never be more than temporary. You've got to fix the cause of the outcome!

For me this meant my lack of consistent success with creating what I wanted in life had to do with the fact that I was pushing around the effects expecting a change that was never going to happen.

Trying to change your circumstances without being aware of your state of being is only expanding more opportunities to experience more of your current state of being. And if you don't like your current state of being, why would you want to experience more of that?

So the next question became…

4. If I'm not particularly enjoying the states of being I'm currently experiencing, or the manifestations they are bringing me, how do I choose the ones I want to experience and have them manifest what I want?

This of course is the million dollar question and the answer I wanted to hear was, "Just choose the ones you want!" But that wasn't it; I'd tried that, it didn't work.

Have you been successful saying, "Okay, even though I am experiencing anger right now, I'm just going to choose happiness"? That's a pretty big leap especially with all the thoughts and feelings that are coursing through your mind and body in that moment.

So simply *choosing* isn't really effective. Another strategy I would employ when I was experiencing thoughts and feelings I really didn't want to be experiencing was to resist them. I'm sure you know how successful that strategy was for me because I'm sure you've experienced it yourself. Here's how a typical conversation of the mind would go employing this strategy...

"Stop being hateful."

"But what a jerk!"

"It's not okay to hate."

"But if I don't hate what he said, aren't I saying that I agree with what he said?"

"You know it's not okay to hate."

"Now I'm just angry and frustrated."

"If you are angry and frustrated you are not vibrating at a matching level with what you want."

"Oh my God—I have to stop thinking and feeling this way."

"But I can't, and now I hate that I can't stop thinking and feeling this way!"

Okay, I think we can agree with the old adage, "What you resist persists" and that it is not a strategy that will work when trying to choose the states of being we want to experience.

I realized that I had spent a lot of time running away from, or resisting certain states of being—hate, fear, failure. I had also spent a lot of time chasing other states of being like happiness, wealth, abundance, and joy.

Well, if I'm resisting in one direction and trying to chase in another, the only place I could end up is stuck between the two. And remember, these states of being exist inside of us right now, so you can't out run them and there is no reason to chase them, they are already there.

If resisting states of being I didn't want to experience expanded my experience with them, then it was time again to consider the opposite—What if I *accepted* my state of being instead of resisting it?

Why not?

I gave it a try.

The first thing I noticed was that when I accepted my state of being, instead of resisting it, I was able to move through it. This was only one of the many benefits I started to experience.

Others included the natural *reduction* of the states of being I had been running from like stress, fear, worry, lack, uncertainty, and the natural *expansion* into the states of beings I had been chasing, like happiness, wealth, health, abundance, knowing, confidence.

So far, by being *willing to consider*, I had uncovered the truth of our creative power:

- States of being—what we ultimately

want—exist inside of us right now and are the creative *cause* of the physical experiences we want to create.

▪ We are the experiencer and we are constantly—consciously or unconsciously— choosing states of being that are manifesting as our thoughts, feelings, words, actions, and physical reality. We are the *master* of our states of being and they are the cause of everything else in our experience.

The words, "consciously or unconsciously" should have caught your eye. If we've been unconscious of our states of being and our power to choose them, it would stand to reason we would not be experiencing everything we want. What's the solution? *Learn how to consciously choose. Fair warning…consciously choosing is a lot different from just "choosing."*

—Chapter 2
Your Foundation For Conscious Creation

Most would think that Superman's super powers would include bending steel, x-ray vision, and an ability to fly, to name just a few. But if Superman wasn't aware that he had these powers, could he use them? If he wasn't **aware** that he could bend steel, it would never occur to him to bend steel. Without awareness, he wouldn't have full access to his abilities.

Here you are with the ability to create your own reality, but because you aren't aware, and are therefore using your power *unconsciously*, you get a mixed bag of results.

Awareness is your power. Once you are aware, you can consciously create the reality you want.

What do you need to be aware of? Your *state of being*, because that is the only thing that is creating your reality. When you are aware, then you can make another choice. Without awareness you are stuck recreating the same reality over and over again.

Right now, what happens for most of us is we look out at reality and say, "That out there makes me angry." Well we've just unconsciously chosen to expand our experience of anger by unconsciously choosing the state of being of anger

In addition, we just let our creation, *reality*, tell us what we are going to create next, more opportunities to experience anger. Not a good plan if we want to experience happiness and peace, and therefore create a reality with physical experiences that expand happiness and peace.

The way you enact your power is simple— Awareness is listening. Listening to what? Your feelings, thoughts, words, and actions. Why? Because they point you back to the state of being you've chosen, the state of being that is manifesting your current experience.

In every moment we have a choice, we can *believe* our feelings, thoughts, words, and actions or we can *listen* to them. Remember, we are the experiencer choosing a state of being, the cause of our experience. Believing the effect wouldn't make much sense if we want to create a new experience.

You know how believing your thoughts and feelings goes...

"I can't believe that jerk cut me off. How unsafe! He could have caused an accident. I bet I'm going to be late. If I'm late I know my boss is going to be mad yet again. What is her problem anyway? Doesn't she understand what it's like to get kids out the door in the morning? Susie is driving me crazy with her inability to

get her homework done. I'm going to have to have a talk with her when I get home. I wonder what time I'll even get home. I'm sick of working such long hours. It's too much pressure!!! When am I going to fit in the grocery store? Bob better have those garbage cans out by the time I get home!!!!"

Fun, huh? No, not really, but isn't that what we do? Imagine the nonsense you would hear if you actually listened to your thoughts instead of believing them.

Believing your thoughts and feelings is like being pulled down a raging river, you are out of control and at the mercy of the river.

What if instead, at the moment you were cut off, you were *aware* and chose to *listen* to your feelings, thoughts, words, and actions? If you were listening to your feelings you would have felt the anger in your body. If you were listening to your thoughts you would have heard yourself lash out at the other driver. What would this have told you? That you had unconsciously chosen the *state of being* of anger.

Some of you might say that the fact that you were cut off *caused* the state of being of anger. Not the case. Why is it that one day someone cuts you off and you send them love and light and another day you want to run them off the road

Your reaction has nothing to do with the

circumstance. It has to do with the *state of being* you had chosen *prior* to the circumstance. I bet you had to read that twice but if you think about it, it makes sense.

Thoughts are easy to listen to, but what about feelings? Just as easy. Try this simple experiment...

I am going to give you a statement to say. I want you to say it out loud, with conviction. As you say it, pay attention to what physically/biologically happens in your body

Okay, say, "I AM RESISTANCE!"

What happened in your body? Did you feel a tightening in your stomach, or tension in your shoulders, or a tightening around your heart? These are just a few examples. Your experience could have been quite different.

Now, I'm going to give you another statement and I want you to do the exact same thing, pay attention to what physically/biologically happens in your body

Okay, say, "I AM ACCEPTANCE

What happened in your body? Did you experience an expansion in your stomach, a loss of tension in your body, a feeling of floating?

Now you know what it is like to listen to your feelings. Your body is always manifesting the state of being you are experiencing, so simply listen to it!

How do you listen to your words? Listen to what you are saying! "I can't," or "It's impossible," or "That will never happen," or "I would love to, BUT." All of these words are being manifested from a state of being of limitation.

How do you listen to your actions? Well if someone cuts you off and you give them the finger you can be pretty sure that that action manifested from a state of being of *anger*. Something more subtle might be if you have decided to lose weight and you find yourself sitting on your couch in front of the TV eating a bag of Cheetos. Your action might be manifesting from a state of being of *doubt* or *frustration*.

It is crucial you remember that what you feel, think, say, or do is not *good* or *bad*. They are physical manifestations of the state of being you have chosen. You are the experiencer, free to experience any state of being and its subsequent effect. So while you may consider that acceptance feels good and resistance feels bad they actually don't, they are simply effects! The state of being of *judgment* creates the thought, "That feels bad."

So your true super power is awareness. Go back to being in the raging river. Awareness is like being in that river, grabbing a branch and pulling yourself out. Once safely on the shore you can just watch the river go by, you are now in control and no longer a victim of the river. Same thing with your thoughts and feelings!

Now, what do you do once you are aware—

listening to your feelings, thoughts, words, and actions? You identify the state of being that created them. Congratulations, you are now officially conscious!

But how do you identify your state of being?

First, you want to be sure that when you identify your state of being you are using the *noun* form of the word. I know, it sounds a bit noodgy, but it is an important distinction.

You are the experiencer choosing the state of being and that state of being is manifesting as your feelings, thoughts, words, actions, and reality. Therefore the state of being of happiness (noun), manifests as a happy (adjective) feeling, a happy thoughts, a happy word, happy actions, and a perception of a happy reality. States of being are "things" (i.e. "nouns") that you are choosing, they are not who you are. They are a cause that causes an effect.

Before I list some examples of states of being, here are some important points to remember about them.

- States of being are dualistic: abundance and lack are two sides of the same coin. It's impossible to experience them at the same time.
- States of being fall into two overall categories: either *acceptance* states of being or *resistance* states of being.

And this the most important point...

- States of being are just states of being. One is not better than another, one is not good or bad, one is not positive and another negative. They are just states of being doing a job, manifesting what *you* chose for them to manifest.

So yes, love is no different from hatred, they just yield different results. You may say, "But I don't want to experience hatred." I get it, neither do I, but the more I resist hatred, by not wanting to experience it, the more I am choosing for it to expand into my experience. *So love and hatred have to be neutral in order for me to be free to choose any state of being.*

This final point is so critical to remember for it is the state of being of judgment that says a state of being is either bad or good and that is why we stay in the cycle of resisting the "bad" ones and chasing after the "good" ones and therefore never experiencing what we want

Our job is to choose the ones that will manifest the experiences we want. Our job is not to fight or struggle with any state of being! Why would a master ever fight with a servant?

So here is a starter list of states of being.

Acceptance states of being…

- Happiness
- Love

- Abundance
- Knowing
- Certainty
- Peace
- Understanding

And some resistance states of being...

- Frustration
- Hatred
- Lack
- Confusion
- Doubt
- Limitation
- Anger
- Judgment

To create in a new direction you have to be willing to make three powerful new choices, the first of which is to...

- Choose to *be aware* and identify your state of being. If you choose not to be aware you will continue to recreate your current experience over and over again by default. You probably feel as though this is the case already.

Choice number two...

- Choose to *accept* your current state of being. This is how you change your creative direction and start creating something new!

How does accepting your state of being change your direction? Because when you become conscious of your state of being and realize that you've been choosing states of being that aren't in alignment with what you want, the last thing you want to do—for reasons we mentioned before—is resist the state of being you are currently experiencing.

A client of mine told me about how she had lost her watch. This wasn't just any watch, it is a very expensive watch, one that is even insured.

At first my client experienced states of being of panic and fear which manifested thoughts about how she would have to contact the insurance company and explain it to them, which manifested thoughts of how she would have to tell so-and-so..... Hence, more panic and fear.

All the while she was looking for her watch. Was it any wonder she wasn't finding it? During this time she checked in her purse, no watch.

Then she *became aware* and started *accepting* her states of being of fear and panic. She kept accepting her states of being and continued looking. Then the thought came in so clearly that she even said it out loud to the person helping her, "I know it is in this house somewhere." Then, without even thinking, she reached back into her purse and pulled out her watch!

Do you see how her states of being of fear and panic kept expanding opportunities to experience more fear and panic which manifested as not being able to find the watch. Do you also see how her states of being of fear and panic manifested thoughts that supported fear and panic?

What happened when she accepted her states of being? Her thoughts supported acceptance and her actions lead her to experience more states of being of acceptance which manifested as the watch being found where she had already looked for it!

When you accept your current state of being you are consciously choosing the state of being of acceptance. When you consciously choose the state of being of acceptance, you are choosing to experience all the acceptance states of being, which are in alignment with manifesting everything you want, and even the things you don't even know that you want.

How do you accept your current state of being? It's easy...

- You are aware
- You identify your state of being
- You say... *"I accept that I am experiencing (insert state of being) right now, and it's okay."*

Let me break this statement down so that you are clear on how to apply it.

- "I accept..." When you say, "I accept" you are **consciously** choosing to manifest the state of being of *acceptance,* which is in alignment with everything that you want to create. You might be thinking that you don't want to accept that you are experiencing failure, but you have to remember that when you accept that you are experiencing failure you are in essence choosing to put failure down and pick up success.

- "that I'm experiencing..." Not, "I am feeling," or "I am thinking," since these are the *effects.* We want to deal with *cause.* I am the experiencer choosing a state of being.

- "the state of being..." The state of being is the thing, the noun, the cause. So "I'm experiencing fear," not "I'm afraid," or "I'm experiencing happiness," not "I am happy." We deal with cause—the state of being—not the effect, the thought, or feeling.

- "right now..." Great reminder that everything is temporary and that you are initiating a change by accepting your state of being.

- "and it's okay." Never drop this last piece; it is the link back to what acceptance really is.

Acceptance is **not** saying that "I will never experience anger again." It is saying that, "Anger is here, and it's okay, it can't hurt me." It is also saying,

"Happiness is here right now and I don't have to hold onto it

As I've mentioned, you are free to choose any state of being. By saying that you will never experience anger you are in direct resistance to it, therefore it has to manifest. If you try to hold onto something you are in resistance to not having it, so that's what you create. Finally, if you say that you can never experience something, or that you have to hold onto something, then you are no longer free.

So why "acceptance." Why not just choose happiness? Two reasons, one makes sense and one is a bit of a paradox.

The first reason: It is hard to just choose happiness when you are knee-deep in anger. I think we have all tried and failed with this one.

The second reason: When you choose something *else* you are actually resisting what is and when you resist what is, you are still manifesting the state of being that created what is. For example, if you were experiencing anger and you wanted to experience happiness, you are in resistance to the experience of anger and since you are experiencing the state of being of anger, it will continue to manifest, no matter what you think you are choosing.

These two reasons are what makes acceptance so powerful. By accepting you are not "faking" or resisting your current experience and are therefore able to easily change your creative direction.

How does your creative direction change by just accepting your state of being? Your state of being manifests as your feelings, thoughts, words, and actions. When you consciously choose acceptance you are choosing for acceptance to start manifesting your feelings, thoughts, words, and actions.

My client came to me to find out more about how he could use the principle of acceptance to change his financial situation. He was in debt, a lot of debt, and had no idea how he was going to pay it off. He had collectors calling for payments in the $1000s. Fear was waking him up at night and he was consumed by the feeling that he had no idea what to do.

My client and I spoke and because he was at the end of his rope, he was completely open to trying anything. He chose to accept his current states of being, which helped him to stop blaming himself for his current situation

Once he was experiencing acceptance he was then able to create a vision of what he wanted to experience next, himself debt free and having extra money to enjoy his life. By continuing to accept the states of being of stress and fear he naturally let go of the "how" his new vision was going to happen and became the person who was already living the vision.

The next day my client was talking with his friend about their season tickets and who was going to go to the next game. They started to argue a bit and my client decided that the tickets weren't worth a rift in their friendship. He told his friend that he was going to sell the tickets. His friend offered him face value for them, $7,500

My client, now manifesting acceptance, was inspired to check the open market. His tickets were worth $70,000 and that's exactly what he sold them for! This paid off all his debt and left him a cushion for enjoying life a bit more!

Now, at first glance you may be amazed about the fact that $70,000 came into his experience, but that is not the amazing part of this story. It is *so* important to recognize that the only thing that changed in my client's experience was his state of being.

He was sitting on these tickets the whole time, but in a state of being of fear, self-loathing, and dissatisfaction, he was unable to see the possibility that he could actually have what he really wanted. He was creating—through his state of being—more of what he didn't want, no way out. His mind was closed down to the fact that he had a valuable asset at his fingertips that he could use to create his vision

My client changed what he was "being" from fearful and trying to control the how, by accepting and being in the moment which changed his direction and got him completely in alignment with what he wanted, being debt free!

How can you be aware and accept?

You choose to be aware and you hear the thought, "I never have enough time." You identify that you are experiencing a state of being of limitation. You say, "I accept that I am experiencing limitation right now, and that's okay."

What will start to happen, if you are willing to continue accepting your state of being, is the state of acceptance will start manifesting as thoughts like, "Maybe I could make it in time." It might manifest as a feeling of confidence that you will make it on time. It might manifest as an action where you leave earlier to ensure that you are on time. The main point is, acceptance will start to manifest through you which will lead to a new experience of you actually being on time— or it not mattering that you weren't!

I mentioned that there were three choices to make in order to create in a new direction. The first two were...

1. Choose to be aware and identify your state of being. If you choose not to be aware you will continue to recreate your current experience over and over again. You probably feel as though this is the case already.

2. Choose to accept your current state of being.

This is how you change creative direction and start creating something new!

And the third?

3. Continue to listen and accept your state of being!

Your commitment to the third step will ensure that your creative direction remains in alignment with what you want

Let's go back to the example of being cut off in traffic and demonstrate what it would be like to be aware and accept.

"I can't believe that jerk cut me off. *(I accept that I am experiencing anger right now, that's okay.)* How unsafe! *(I accept I'm experiencing fear right now, that's okay.)* He could have caused an accident. *(I accept I'm experiencing fear right now, it's okay.)* I bet I'm going to be late. *(I accept I'm experiencing worry right now, it's okay.)* If I'm late I know my boss is going to be mad yet again. *(I accept I'm experiencing worry right now, and it's okay.)* What is her problem anyway? *(I accept I'm experiencing judgment right now, it's okay.)* Doesn't she understand what it's like to get kids out the door in the morning? *(I accept I'm experiencing judgment right now, it's okay.)* Susie is driving me crazy with her inability to get her homework done. *(I accept I'm experiencing frustration right now, it's okay.)* I'm going to have to have a talk with her when I get home. *(I accept I'm experiencing resistance right now, it's okay.)* I wonder what time I'll even get home. *(I accept I'm experiencing confusion right now, it's okay.)* I'm sick of working such long hours. *(I accept I'm experiencing frustration right now, it's okay.)* It's too much pressure!!! *(I accept I'm experiencing stress right now, it's okay.)* When am I going to fit in the grocery store? *(I accept I'm experiencing confusion right now, it's okay.)* Bob better have those garbage cans out by the time I get home!!!! *(I accept I'm experiencing anger right now, it's okay.)"*

This was just an example so you can see how being aware and accepting your state of being works. In reality, the direction of your thoughts would have changed early on in the example because you were choosing acceptance and it would start to manifest as thoughts of clarity, peace, and possibility.

Here is a client example of how your thoughts naturally change direction according to the state of being you choose in the moment.

"Yesterday I had the most incredible internal shift. Here is how it went. I was moving through my day and I became aware that I was in that robotic, trance-like place. So...I asked myself 'what are you experiencing right now in this moment?' Flat, mundane. 'I accept that I am experiencing flatness/mundaneness right now and that's ok.' I waited to see what came next. Worry about my daughter came next. I accepted that I was

experiencing worry and that it was ok. I caught myself a few times drifting off into conversation with the worried thought. The worried thought and I were discussing ways I could perhaps fix/change my daughters' circumstances (pretty wild since I can't even change my own). But then I remembered what Doreen said about having a thought as opposed to believing a thought. Doreen said 'How do you know when you are believing a thought? You know when you are having a conversation with it!' That awareness ended the conversation with the worried thought. I reminded myself that the worried thoughts I was experiencing about my daughter's life and happiness were the effects of my state of being. I kept accepting the worry. Then I realized that my state of being when it comes to my kids is almost always worry. And, like, they're grown ups!!! This awareness blew me away cuz I swear on a stack of Bibles y'all, I was unaware of this. Much as I adore my daughters and think they are awesome and enjoy them, I worry about them all the time. Have for their whole life and so I always tried hard to do whatever I could to make their life good. And of course, since I can't always do that (that power ended when they were about one), I just worry and hope they are ok. I have to check on them ALL the time to see if they are still ok!!!! Then it occurred to me that their life was their own and that I was even judging their life. I became willing to consider that they belonged to LIFE and like a seed planted in the ground, would become what it would. The next thing that came in was the most wonderful feeling of freedom. I accept I am experiencing freedom and that's ok. Then I had such an experience of understanding. I got it! Thoughts, feelings, circumstances are INFORMATION!!!!! Mirrors!!!! So then I experienced such appreciation for the awareness I do have. I have learned how to read life's messages!!! Doreen had responded to one of my questions a while back by telling me that it did not matter that I experienced fear/lack/worry all of the time. What mattered was that I was aware of it. And that's why whatever I am experiencing is really, really ok!!!! By the way, in the middle of typing this the daughter I was worried about called to tell me about a decision she made and how good and empowered she was feeling!!!!"

Do you see that my client's state of being of worry was not in alignment with her desire to see her children as safe and powerful? Once she started accepting she quickly got in alignment and her feelings and thoughts changed to reflect her new direction and her desire.

You are probably thinking, "Good God, that's a lot of work!" Of course becoming conscious is a lot of work when you've been unconscious for so long.

But try to think of it this way....I put you in front of a locked door. Behind the door is everything you ever wanted, and I mean *everything*! I hand you a key and instruct you to use it to open the door, go through the door, grab one thing that you want, then come back through the door. The door will lock again. Then I tell you that you can use the key as often as you like to go and get whatever you want. How many times do you think you will use the key? A bazillion comes to my mind.

The state of being of acceptance is the key that keeps opening the door by keeping you in creative alignment with what you want. Bottom line, if you want love, health, wealth, and purpose you will never experience them by choosing states of being of hatred, lack, and limitation.

So is the work worth it? I would say so, but you will have to determine that for yourself. What I can tell you is once you start choosing acceptance and expanding acceptance you will start to experience more peace, health, wealth, happiness and abundance. You have to because you are consciously choosing to!

My client went to see his accountant. He had filed an extension on his taxes and was in the middle of getting all his paperwork together. At the meeting his account ran the numbers and said that at this point it looked as though Wayne would owe the government $3,000. Keep in mind, my client had been recently laid off from his job.

With that said, he had been accepting his state of being and had been experiencing peace about his current employment status and excitement about his prospects. He left his accountant and diligently accepted all the states of being that came up, lack, fear, scarcity doubt. Then the thought came in, "Wouldn't it be nice if the government owed me $3,000 instead?"

Obviously this thought was a clear reflection that he was experiencing acceptance, or else he never would have even had it. Wayne kept accepting as he pulled together the remainder of the paperwork. He kept accepting as he was sitting with the accountant for the final figure. He kept accepting and the final figure was actually $17,000, THAT THE GOVERNMENT OWED HIM!

My client had been expanding acceptance and it created a result that he could never have imagined. What result do you think he would have experienced had he been experiencing resistance? Bottom line, my client has been experiencing possibility and possibility became his reality.

Before we move on, here are some more tips on accepting...

- Don't *qualify* your state of being. It is just a state of being. For instance, you don't need to say, "I accept I'm experiencing *intense* fear right now, and that's okay." Remember, as the experiencer you are simply experiencing a state of being. Be sure not to make it anything more than it is. By saying it is "intense" you are judging it to be way more than it is. So, "I accept I'm experiencing fear right now, that's okay."

- Don't make it about physical reality. "I accept that I'm experiencing anger *that Jimmy isn't focused on his homework,* right now, that's okay." State of being is cause, so the circumstance—Jimmy not doing what you want him to do—is merely a reflection of the current state of being of anger. There is no reason to bring in the effect, when we are focused on accepting the cause. So, "I accept I'm experiencing anger right now, that's okay."

- Don't drop, "...it's okay." When you say, "I accept I'm experiencing fear right now," the final part, "...and that's okay" is really important because that is what acceptance is. It's the understanding that even though you are experiencing fear, you are okay. So it doesn't matter if you experience fear ever again, you know that no matter what, you ARE OKAY!! So, the magic phrase is, "I accept I am experiencing fear right now, that's okay."

- Don't bring in the effect. "I accept that I am *feeling* anger right now, that's okay." If state of being is cause, then a feeling is the effect, caused by the state of being that you are experiencing. Remember, you are the experiencer, not the state of being. So you want to say, "I accept I'm *experiencing* anger right now, that's okay." Notice how with every example we always use the same acceptance phrase? It really is that simple, be sure to keep it that way.

- Don't make it about "feeling good." Think about a roller coaster and at the end of the track is the experience you want. You start out of the gate going straight then you start to go up and then you go down. Up and down, up and down, until finally you get to the end and you experience what you want. The ups and downs are due to you trying to feel better.

Now imagine if the roller coaster didn't go up and down and just made a beeline to the end, the experience you want. You would experience what you want faster. That's what acceptance does, it keeps you on the straight track to what you want.

The goal isn't to "feel good." The goal is to consciously choose acceptance so that you create the experiences you want, and then *you feel good naturally* because you are experiencing what you want. If you make it about feeling good then you are choosing the ups and downs of the roller coaster ride and it will simply take you longer to have what you desire.

For those of you who feel like you are a victim of your thoughts and that you have no control over them, by being aware and accepting you will have proof that you don't have to be pulled along by your thoughts

Here's why. Can you physically say two things at once? Nope, not possible.

Well guess what? You can't think two thoughts at once either. I know it can sometimes feel as though you are having a million thoughts at a time, but it's not physically possible. When you listen for one thought at a time, identify your state of being and accept it, you are actually slowing down your thinking! This will be a great relief to a lot of you out there. I know it was to me.

The other good news is that you can also only experience one state of being at a time so identifying them will be easy if you keep your attention on one at a time

The biggest benefit of being conscious is that you get to create the life you want, not just the life you think you can have.

The following points are the foundation of creating consciously. All that follows won't matter if you don't remember that...

- States of being, what we ultimately want, exist inside of us right now and are the creative cause of the physical experiences we want to create.

- We are the experiencer and we are constantly—consciously or unconsciously—choosing states of being that are manifesting as our thoughts, feelings, words, actions, and physical reality. We are the master of our states of being and they are the cause of everything else in our experience.

You can move from unconscious creating to conscious creating by:

1. Choosing to be aware and identify your state of being.

2. Choosing to accept your current state of being.

3. Choosing to *continue* to listen and accept your state of being!

Now that your foundation is rock solid, let's move on to how you can use conscious creation to create the actual experiences you want.

—Chapter 3

Setting Your Creative Stage

We have what we ultimately want—the state of being we want to experience—inside of us right now. We are now consciously choosing acceptance so we are not only experiencing the *states of being* we want, we are also in alignment with the *experiences* we want to create.

How can we create the physical circumstances we know will expand our desired experiences? First and foremost you have to be willing to get clear on what it is you actually want to experience.

Getting Clear

First thing first. Decide what you want. Is it more business, a new career, your soul mate, more time to be with your family, a better relationship with your child, more opportunities to travel, a goal you've always wanted to achieve, or to break through to the next level of success? Is it your ideal home, a car you've always wanted, or a wardrobe you always wished for? It doesn't matter, just get clear and choose.

Why is it so important to get clear? Because you have the right to be, do, and have anything, but if you don't know what "that" is, you can't be headed in the right direction. Plus how will you know that you got "it" if you don't know what "it" is?

How clear do you need to be? As clear as you are right now. Sometimes you will be very clear. I decided that from now on I wanted to work with my ideal clients. So I wrote a list of what these ideal clients would look like. They would...

- Be fun, energetic, excited
- Apply what they learn
- Be authentic and honest
- Want my business to succeed
- Share their experiences and results
- Refer me to like-minded folks
- Pay upfront without question because they easily recognize the value of my work
- Be without excuses
- Be good listeners
- Be excited to get to the next level
- Be a cheerleader for me and my business

Sometimes you will feel as though you have no clue what you want next. My client feared she wasn't clear on what she wanted next. I said, "It seems to be you want to do work you love with art and music while making a great living doing it." She was very pleased that she did in fact know that much. She had a direction now!

You only know what you know right now, but with acceptance that will expand exponentially, so just start with what you know right now. That's all it takes to get started!

I'll use the example *to start a business.* I think a lot of us would enjoy the freedom of running our own business doing something we really love.

This is a good time to point out the importance of identifying *what* you want, not *how* you think you are going to get it. The only thing you create when you consciously create is the end result, you do not create the "how."

How can I be so sure of this? Ask yourself, "Have I planned every single thing that has happened in my lifetime?" Of course not! How many times in your life have you gotten something you wanted in a totally unexpected way? The "how" of how that happens is the universe's job.

"Hi Doreen,

I thought I would share something that happened to me today along the lines of focusing on your end result, not the "how" and staying in acceptance.

A couple of weeks ago I thought it would be a good idea to reach out to PGA golfer Matt Kuchar to see if he had an interest in my coaching program for athletes. I saw Matt interviewed and he believes in the correct mindset and staying in the moment while competing. I did some research online, found his agent and sent them an email & letter discussing my program with the potential of us doing something together. The assistant called me and said they received the letter and would forward it on to Matt.

This morning I was driving to get a cup of coffee and I pulled up to Panera but the lot was crowded and it forced me to park in the next lot by Starbucks. I was on the phone so I sat in my car for a minute and I saw a PGA courtesy car pull up. A woman got out of the passenger side and walked into Starbucks. The PGA event is in Chicago this week, not far from me, so I figured this was a golfer with the courtesy car.

I hung up the phone and walked past the car to see who the golfer was and it looked like...Matt Kuchar! He had a hat on and his head was down so I walked into Starbucks and figured I would ask his wife before I freaked him out by walking up to his car. She was very nice and I asked her if that was Matt in the car. She said, yes it was. I explained to her who I was and the fact that I sent him an email a few weeks ago. She told me to go say hi, that Matt would be happy to speak with me.

I walked to the car. Matt rolled down his window and I made introductions. He was very nice, said he remembered seeing something about my email but hadn't had time to respond yet. I told him a little about my program along with telling him I would love to do something together. We spoke a bit, I gave him my card and he said he would be in touch.

It's really funny how my morning played out: I was delayed by a phone call, then by someone at the gas station, but I ended up pulling into Starbuck's the same time as Matt Kuchar...very cool. I'm not sure where this will lead nor do I have to know right now but, just more confirmation of how things work when you focus on your desired end result and remain in acceptance.

~ Mike"

My client has a band. Her bass player got some dates mixed up in her calendar and realized that she would be unable to make it to TWO of their gigs! The other band members went into panic, but my client had acceptance on her side and was able to keep her attention on the end result she wanted, having a substitute bass player for these two upcoming gigs.

Her next thought was to call another bass player she knew. When she called, she was told that that person wasn't there, but there was a different bass player she could speak with.

He jumped on the phone, she explained what she needed, and he said, "You're never going to believe this, but I literally just had cancellations for both of those dates!!" My client did her job, she stayed clear on what she wanted by accepting her states of being and the universe did its job for both her and the bassist.

So stay focused on your job and just get clear. Define the end result: "I am in business for myself doing work I love and making a great living." It's fine to add more specifics if you know them, but really it is that simple. You only know what you know right now, so start there and you will know more very quickly.

What will get in your way of clarity? Possibly one of these several obstacles, all of them manifested from states of being of *resistance:*

- The state of being of **need** will manifest an end result that reflects something you think you "need" in order to have what you ultimately want. The most obvious example of this is when we think we "need" money in order to buy the car, go on the vacation, get the education, and so on. If I came to your door and said, "I'm here to give you your dream vacation to Italy you've always wanted," would you say, "Thanks but no, I want to earn the money for it first." Probably not. (Well I certainly hope you wouldn't say that!) You want to have your attention on the end result, not what you "think" you "need" to experience it.

  One of my clients gave quite a list of what she thought she needed regarding what she wanted, to share her love of raw food. She thought she had to own a restaurant, go to school, get certified, do wellness classes.

I was starting to get overwhelmed and so was she. I could hear it in her voice. I then asked her what her heart wanted to do next and she said she wanted to do a raw food dinner party, take on-line classes, and buy a Cuisinart. She sounded much more excited about working on these next steps. That's how we knew she was on the right path: it felt *naturally* good.

If your end result is manifested from a state of being of need, you will only manifest more need. You will *need* to do more things before you can experience what you want. By the way, my client did have her first dinner party and is now leading "Green Smoothie Cleansing" retreats in Australia and Thailand.

▪   The state of being of **limitation** will manifest end results that you think you "can" have, not necessarily what you really *want* to have. This is the definition of settling and it's not a way to live!

I had a client tell me a list of what he wanted. He gave me an exhaustive list which, to be honest, I was quite bored with. Then finally, to my relief, his last desire was to be a race car driver. All the way at the bottom of the list! I asked him out of all the things he listed, what did he REALLY want to do. You guessed it, be a race car driver.

One thing I can guarantee you is that if you aren't honest about what you want, you will *never* experience it! Conversely, if you are honest, there is no way you can't experience it, if you stick with it until it happens. My client? Yep, he's racing cars!

- The state of being of **confusion** will manifest more confusion, or more not knowing what you want. This one is pretty self-evident.

What do you do to bypass these obstacles? Be aware and accept your state of being. When you accept that you are experiencing *need* you open up to fulfillment. When you accept that you are experiencing *limitation*, you open up to possibility. When you accept that you are experiencing *confusion* you open up to clarity. Then you will open up to and be honest about the end result you really want.

I almost forgot to share with you what happened when I got honest and clear on my ideal client. The next day I was sitting in Starbucks doing some work when two women sat down next to me. They struck up a conversation with me and I ended up telling them I wrote a book on the Law of Attraction. One of the women said that her business partner loved the Law of

Attraction and she couldn't wait to tell her about me.

Well she did and asked if we could meet. I said of course and two days later we met at Starbucks. Well, Maureen and I locked eyes and we didn't come up for air for over an hour. We talked about the Law of Attraction, her business, my book. She asked if I would be willing to do some training for her team which I was happy to do.

Finally, at the end of the conversation, she asked if I did anything besides writing and training and I told her I was a Life Coach. Her jaw dropped and she told me that not too long ago she decided she wanted to work with someone, a coach, to take her to the next level. She hired me on the spot!

Maureen fit every quality on my ideal client list and more, a lot more. She and her family have become my family and she has enriched my life beyond anything I could have imagined.

The benefit of being clear on what you want is that it will lead you to what you want, and in a lot of cases, well beyond what you thought you wanted.

Getting Unstuck

Okay, once you define the end result it's time to get an understanding of why it is you aren't already enjoying the end result right now. Either it's because this is a new idea you've only had recently and it just hasn't manifested yet or more likely it's because you are stuck.

What causes something to get stuck in the physical world? *Resistance.* When things meet resistance nothing moves. Water moves and continues to move until something resists it. Then, (as long as there is not another path for it to take) it stays stuck and gets stagnant. When two people argue and resist each other, neither of their agendas can move forward. Their agendas get and stay stuck.

What causes you to get and stay stuck? Initially you might think that circumstances cause you to be stuck, but that's not true. People have experienced the same circumstances and are not stuck. Just like the physical world, you are stuck because you are experiencing resistance, the state of being. This state of being is manifesting as all the reasons you think you are stuck and therefore your circumstances reflect more resistance, more *stuck.*

The only way to get unstuck is to change the cause of being stuck, resistance. How? By accepting that you are experiencing it. I know, you may be thinking that you should do the opposite and resist the resistance. By now, though, you know that resisting it will only expand it.

How is resistance manifesting for someone who is stuck? It's manifesting as one insidious word responsible for killing countless dreams..."but."

"I would really like to own my own business, BUT..."

As soon as you say "but" you slam the door on your end result. You went from acceptance to resistance in one sentence. Now your mind can only manifest all the reasons why you can't have a business.

Whenever you hear the word "but" you are experiencing resistance, more specifically in this instance, you are experiencing a state of being of impossibility. First things first, *accept your state of being!*

Once you accept your state of being then the "buts" are worth taking a look at because as you will see they are easy—especially when you are accepting—to move past. Here's how you do it.

Take a piece of paper and write your desire at the top of it. Then draw a vertical line down the middle of the paper creating two columns. The left-hand column will be your "But" column. Start here. Write all your "Buts." For our example, it might go like this: "I would really like to own my own business, BUT..."

- I don't have any business experience
- I don't even know what kind of business I want to run
- It will take a lot of money to get a business going

- There is too much competition out there
- Who am I to run my own business
- My partner will think I'm crazy
- I don't even have the time to think of running a business

That's a good start. Now let's take a look at what these buts really are. First, who's in charge of what you believe? Can anyone other than yourself be in charge of what you personally believe? Impossible. You are the only one who will ever be in charge of what you believe.

So, ask yourself, "Why do I believe things I don't really want to believe?" Think you don't? Look at that list of "buts." They are your current beliefs—thoughts created by the state of being of resistance—that you've thought over and over again.

Do you really *want* to believe that you can't have what you want? I'm not asking you if you believe you can't have what you want, I'm asking you if you *want* to believe that you can't. Of course you don't. Then why do you choose to believe all of your "buts?" Let's get you on track with considering some new beliefs.

The right-hand column on your paper is your "I'm willing to consider" column. Look at each "but" you've written and ask yourself, "What do I really want to believe here?"

So our example would go like this...

- I don't have any business experience. *I'm*

willing to consider I could get the experience I need.

- I don't even know what kind of business I want to run. *I'm willing to consider that I could know what type of business I would like to run.*

- It will take a lot of money to get a business going. *I'm willing to consider that I will figure out the money.*

- There is too much competition out there. *I'm willing to consider that there is plenty of opportunity for everybody.*

- Who am I to run my own business? *I'm willing to consider that I deserve to create anything I want.*

- My partner will think I'm crazy. *I'm willing to consider that my partner could be supportive."*

- I don't even have the time to think of running a business. *I'm willing to consider that I could make the time."*

This is a simple, but powerful exercise. It moves you from the state of being of impossibility to possibility and that's all you need. You just need a little crack in the window of possibility to get started and that crack is you being *willing to consider.*

Be sure to accept your state of being as you write out your "willing to consider" list. You want to experience a sense of acceptance when you write them or else you will be fooling yourself, which is resistance.

Once you've come up with your "willing to considers," then cross out your "buts." You are done with putting attention on them, now it's time for you to get your attention squarely on your, "willing to considers."

Now go back to your end result. Mine was, "I am in business for myself doing work I love and making a great living." Get quiet and just say your end result to yourself. Now be aware. If a "but" comes up, accept that you are experiencing resistance right now and that's okay. Then say, "I'm willing to consider..." Then be aware and listen again.

Accept that state of being and then be willing to consider. By doing this you are choosing the state of being of acceptance that is in alignment with your end result and you are opening up your mind even further to the possibility that you could have exactly what you want.

What happens with this powerful combination? The acceptance starts to manifest and it manifests as ideas, inspirations, and opportunities that will in turn manifest your end result. The *willing to considers* help to keep you focused on what you want, not what you don't want. They also help you gain clarity on what you honestly want, not what you think you "can" have.

Here's how one client used this process to get

clearer. The desire statement was "I want to be a professional writer..." and here's how the "buts" and the "willing to consider" lists unfolded.

- BUT: I am so constrained and limited by my current situation that I can't get out of it. *Do I really want to believe that? No, I really want to believe that the internal creates the external not the other way around.*

- I AM WILLING TO CONSIDER: that circumstances are effects not causes. They cannot stop me doing what I really want to do or becoming who I really am.

- BUT: I have no idea what to write about and haven't written in such a long time that the creative energy within me has dried up. *Do I really want to believe that? No, I really want to believe that the creative energy of the universe is infinite. The way I am feeling now is just a reaction to events and circumstances.*

- I AM WILLING TO CONSIDER: that as a child of the universe I am a legitimate heir to that creative energy and through awareness, acceptance, and allowing I can experience it again and even better than before.

- BUT: I have no experience or contacts in the worlds of publishing, film, and entertainment so I will not be able to make a start in any of those industries. *Do I really want to believe that? No, I really want to believe that possibility and opportunity, like creativity, are unlimited. I have seen other people become successful so there is no reason why I shouldn't also.*

▪ I AM WILLING TO CONSIDER: that the possibility and opportunity to become a professional writer is open to me as well.

This process led my client to…

A description of my dream made real: I am a successful professional writer. My screenplays are made into films which film lovers throughout the world enjoy. I also write for radio and television. My success in these fields has opened up opportunities in related fields such as directing and adapting the work of other writers. Creative energy erupts from me like a fountain and I have more ideas than I know what to do with. Getting started was not a problem as the people who commission new work enjoyed my submissions so much that they were eager to produce them and present them to a bigger audience. My past life of unhappy drudgery was obliterated instantaneously when I became a successful professional writer."

A word of caution

Remember, your *state of being* is what *creates* so don't just replace *awareness* and *acceptance* with *willing to considers.* It won't matter what you are willing to consider if you are saying it in a state of being of resistance!

Also, be sure that you always check in with your state of being even *after* you've stated your *willing to consider* to ensure that you are accepting the true state of being you are experiencing.

Let's take this example: "I am willing to consider I will make the time to start a business." Your next thought might be, "Yeah right, I don't even have enough time to brush my teeth in the morning." Just accept that you are experiencing resistance right now and that's okay. Then listen again and see what comes up. If you are experiencing resistance, just continue to accept and then throw in the willing to consider when you feel as though acceptance is expanding.

Identify the States of Being That will Create the Experience You Want

Since states of being *create* then our job is to know what we want to create and then identify the states of being we would experience when we actually experience the thing we want. So the state of being of...

- Wealth creates more money

- Happiness creates that trip you've been wanting to take
- Success creates more business for you
- Love creates an opportunity to experience your soul mate
- Understanding creates a better relationship with your child
- Prosperity creates the promotion at work

None of the things we want can create themselves, they all come from a state of being you've chosen to experience now that manifests into the thing you want.

Go back to your end result and ask yourself, "What states of being will I experience when I actually have this?"

For the business example I would say, "Now that I am in business for myself doing work I love and making a great living I am experiencing happiness, wealth, success, freedom, and joy." So the states of being that are actually going to create my new business venture are happiness, wealth, success, freedom, and joy. Notice they are all acceptance states of being.

So why aren't I experiencing them right now?

Drop the need

Our conditioning says that we can't experience the state of being unless we actually experience the physical thing. Guess what state of being we are experiencing when you we say we need something in order to have something? NEED. Bottom line, the state of being of need creates more opportunities to need.

I'll bet you can relate to the frustration we've all experienced in the past because we were unaware that we were doing this backwards. We'd say, "I'll be happy when...." What we were actually saying was, "I need ... in order to experience happiness right now." So we just kept creating more need and never a true experience of happiness.

That is why we want to make a conscious effort to drop the need, and it's so easy. Simply say, "I am willing to consider that I don't need (the end result you want) in order to experience (the states of being that will create the end result) right now."

So my business example could be, "I'm willing to consider that I don't need a new business in order to experience happiness, wealth, success, freedom, and joy right now."

By taking this simple step you release the need and are therefore open to experiencing those states of being now which puts you right on track to creating the end result you want.

Here is how one client not only got on track, she actually arrived.

"Not so long ago I emailed you in regards to the

fact that I 'needed' a car for my new business so that I could visit clients. My husband and I shared one car which he used for work. So far this had worked well but circumstances had changed and I really, really needed — not just wanted—a new car. You wrote to me and said:

'Okay, you said it yourself, your state of being is NEED. You want to drop the need so that your state of being can be acceptance. Try this... I am willing to consider that I don't need a car in order to experience (the state of being you are going to experience when you have a car) right now. Your state of being is what is always expanding, so you are expanding need right now. Once you drop the need, as long as your state of being is acceptance when you drop it, then your state of being will expand which would include all the opportunities to have a car.'

So I did and do you know what? I took delivery of my new car a week ago and I am still in shock. I can't believe how easily everything just fell into place. And the funny thing is, I had in my mind the sort of car that I wanted and ended up with something completely different and infinitely better. It hadn't even occurred to me to look at this particular model! The universe obviously had different ideas and I just got out of the way and voila...."

Now the question becomes, "How do you stay on track?"

Be aware and accept your state of being

Awareness and acceptance come full circle. Remember I said acceptance was the foundation of consciously creating? Well this is why.

All the states of being that you are going to experience when you have the end result you want are acceptance states of being. Therefore, every time you choose to accept your state of being you are choosing the states of being that are going to create your end result. You are in direct alignment with the end result you want. In addition, you don't have to wait to experience what you ultimately want, the state of being.

Congratulations you are now...

- Unstuck.
- No longer in "need" of creating the experience you want in order to experience the states of being that will actually create it.
- Knowing the states of being that are going to create what you want.
- Choosing acceptance so that you stay in alignment with what you want.

Now it's time to consciously tie your states of being to a particular experience you want and manifest it into your physical reality.

—Chapter 4
Consciously Creating Your Results

You have set the foundation with your awareness and choosing acceptance. You have gotten clear and unstuck. Now is the time to tie your conscious creative process to an end result you want to experience. This is a powerful two-step process.

Step One: "Spirit becomes what it wants to create."

As I mentioned, a lot, your state of being right now is creating what happens for you next. In order to create what you want, you have to be willing to experience the states of being you think you will experience when you have the thing you want, right now. When you are not experiencing them, then you want to accept the state you *are* experiencing so that you stay in alignment with those creative states as much as possible.

You have an opportunity to consciously connect with these states of being in a very powerful way, a way in which you *actually* experience them, you don't just *say* that you are experiencing them.

In your reading you may have come across the concept of "I AM." Basically, "I AM" is your awareness.

Before you can be happy you have to be aware of YOU, then you become aware of you being happy. So "I AM" is your awareness of being.

"I AM" is you without any qualifications, expectations, beliefs, or perceived identities. It is the pure spiritual "you" before you put any meaning to what you think you are. It is you connected to the whole, at one with everything. It is you, free to be, do, or have anything. "I AM" is basically the REAL you, the experiencer.

This may seem pretty deep for our conversation on consciously creating your reality, but it the most powerful concept for you to understand because whatever you qualify "I AM" as, is what you experience and that is crucial to what you are creating.

When you say things like...

"I am sick."

"I am happy."

"I am tired."

"I am abundant."

"I am poor."

You are typically looking at the current reality and *think* that you are stating a fact. The "fact" is that you are experiencing what you are in that moment because you chose, consciously or unconsciously, to experience those states previous to this moment.

This is going to be weird, but try to understand

that your current reality is actually a past reality you created by choosing your states of being. In essence you can never change your physical reality, you can only create beyond it.

Inventors know exactly what this means. They don't look at their current physical reality and let that tell them that they can't create beyond it. They live and create in the creative reality that lies beyond physical reality.

So our job is to not try to change reality, it is to create what we want which lies beyond our current reality. Any attempt to resist your current reality will hold it in place because your attention can only be on one thing at a time.

Okay, back to connecting with "I AM." Try this exercise:

- Take a moment to get quiet.
- Just listen to each thought that comes up and identify the state of being creating it and accept.
- When your mind settles down and you feel quiet start saying, "I AM." This is you connecting to what you really are, the experiencer. Just say it gently and pay attention to what you feel physically.
- Keep saying it, gently, quietly and see what you feel. Some feel a lifting within them-

selves or a lightness. Some feel an expansion beyond their body. The idea is to pay attention to your experience. If you find nothing happening and you experience frustration then go back to accepting until you quiet down again. Then go back to "I AM."

• Once you experience something, whatever it is to you, you'll know, then start claiming your states of being, the ones you identified you would experience when you are experiencing the thing you want to experience. Claim one at a time. For example, "I AM happiness." *Be sure to remember you are claiming the state of being, not the effect* so it is "happiness," not "happy." Stay with the one you choose, feel it, enjoy it, connect with it. Then move on to the next state of being you identified and so on until you've experienced, and really enjoyed each one.

What I—and my clients—have found is that once you connect with "I AM" by simply stating it, then as soon as you say the state of being you automatically feel it. This means that you have consciously chosen to experience the state of being that will ultimately create the physical experience that you want! Pretty powerful, huh?

Now it is important to not "try" and stay in those states of being. When you "try" you are experiencing resistance and, as you now know, resistance is not in alignment with what you want. So be honest about the state you are experiencing and just accept it. That's how you get back in alignment with the states of being that are creating what you want.

Step Two: Powerful visualization

During your journey I'm sure that you've also come across the idea of visualization. Visualization is powerful because it is another method to get you focused on what you want, not what you don't want. Couple it with "I AM" and you super-charge your creative power.

Once you sit in those amazing states of being for some time during your "I AM" exercise, then you want to "pop" a visualization that represents an event that could only exist because you achieved your end result. For example, if you want a promotion at your job then an event that would follow you actually getting the promotion might be a co-worker congratulating you.

When creating your visualization you want to be sure that you keep it simple and...

- Short—You want to pick one simple event that represents an experience after you get what you want. This will become important when you actually do your visualization. You will be better able to focus on a simple event versus a complex one.

- Visceral—You want to see, hear, taste, and touch in your visualization. The more visceral the better. This is what makes your desire crystal clear to the infinite mind that will create it. It's like giving an exact blueprint to a builder.

- Experiential—*You* are actually experiencing the event, not looking *at* the event. You have to be *in* the event, seeing, touching, tasting, and hearing exactly what you would experience if the event were actually happening to you. So you see the face of your co-worker, you feel their hand in yours, maybe you smell the flowers on your desk that someone sent to congratulate you. So you are *in* the event, like you are remembering it. You're not outside, looking at it.

You will find that the states of being you experience when you are visualizing will be the same states you experienced in your "I AM" exercise. What you are ultimately doing is tying the states of being directly to the event you want to experience, which will create that event, which—since it can only exist after you experience the thing you want—means that you created what you wanted to experience!

Remember my client who wanted to be a writer? Well here's what he developed for his visualization:

"Thank you for your comments. They were very helpful. You're right, I was focusing on the process of writing rather than the end result of me actually being a writer.

Seeing myself writing is not a very inspiring visualization so it isn't surprising I didn't get very far with it. What being a writer would mean to me is the realization of other dreams on my list as well. So I visualized myself living in a modern, architect designed house on the west coast of America with a view of the Pacific Ocean.

Instead of a boring vision of me writing I saw myself floating in my infinity pool enjoying the warmth of the sun, birds wheeling in the blue sky, waves crashing on the shore, a cool drink in my hand as I imagined the characters and dramatic scenarios that would form the basis of my screenplays. Inside the house a pen magically transcribed what I was imagining, the paper folded, enveloped, and mailed itself and by return mail I received a large cheque.

It was fun to do. So much so that I felt myself smiling as I visualized. Once I got started it was amazing how quickly it developed a momentum of its own and because it was fun to do it was easy to repeat it at odd moments throughout the day. It continues to develop. I see myself going to a movie theatre to see a film that I have written. I see myself driving along the Pacific Coast

Highway in a classic convertible. It's all good."

A client who wants to get into a career focused on helping people came up with..."I am being hugged with heartfelt emotions by this person whom I love and cherish dearly. With tears in his eyes, he is telling me how thankful he is for getting him all the help and support he really needed to break free of this debilitating emotional illness which he had believed was permanent and hopeless. He's describing his new life and how happy he is now. I am crying too, as I hear his story and see him this way. My heart is overflowing with joy and gratitude in knowing that what I believed was indeed possible! I did it! I did it! I made my dream real! I am so happy being the creator I knew I could be!!!!!"

And finally a client that wanted a condo... *"I'm driving up to the condo with Theo on Saturday morning—easy drive, no traffic and looking forward to a relaxing weekend. I am in my condo, easing into the day, sipping coffee out on the deck looking out at the lake, relaxing and planning my weekend. I enjoy all that the area has to offer: kayaking, biking and outdoor living. I feel safe, happy and stress free. I can even commute home on Monday morning when there is no traffic."*

All are great examples of short, simple, visceral, and experiential visualizations.

The best time to do this two-step process is in the morning when you wake up and at night before you go to bed. These are quiet moments when the mind is super receptive to what you are consciously suggesting. When you first start out, it is also a good idea to stop in the middle of your day and do this exercise. Remember, you are starting to focus your mind in a different direction. The *states of being* you are now consciously choosing will do this naturally eventually, but you, like most, are probably in need of a jump-start.

I bet you are wondering how long you will need to do this exercise. Well, I trust that you are going to enjoy it. I mean it is all about experiencing wonderful states of being and thinking about something you want as if you are already experiencing it. So, the answer is, *until you experience what you want.*

When you get going with this you may find that this does indeed feel like an "exercise," but eventually you start to feel like it is fun and exciting. In essence you are going from resistance to acceptance regarding what you want to experience. If you are willing to stick with it until you get what you want, then you are guaranteed to get what you want.

Now, what about *action*? This is the fun part!

I know, it seems like we are doing a lot of "mental action", but what about actual "physical actions"?

First of all, everything comes from mental action first. Think about it, until someone chooses a state of being and then has an idea (mental action), no physical action can be taken. All that we see in physical reality came from the invisible. Again, the most obvious proof of this is an invention. I met an inventor once who made a nuclear powered, at this particular stage of his creation, go-cart. His plan was to eventually create a car that worked off this energy. I asked him how long it took to create the go-cart and he said, "Well, it was created in my mind four years ago." Spoken like a true creator!

Since everything comes from state of being, which drives your feelings, thoughts, words, and actions then it stands to reason that mental action, awareness, and consciously choosing acceptance, is more important than any physical action you take. So what physical action *should* we be taking? Inspired action, action that comes from intuition.

I had a conversation with a client who was waiting around for her inspired action. We laughed a little because we both knew this process isn't at all about "waiting around" for anything. Once we stopped laughing, it became clear that there is a distinction to make when it comes to what inspired action really is.

I think there is a myth flying around that inspired action is some mystical guidance that will come to us "when we are ready." This reminds me of a great story in the equally great book, *Eat, Pray, Love.*

The main character is on her bathroom floor in the middle of the night begging God to tell her what to do next to get out of the miserable life she created. And the guidance did come. It told her to "go back to bed." Friends, this is inspired action.

Inspired action is simply any action that feels good and makes the most intuitive sense at the time. The only thing mystical about it is that it feels good and most of us are so used to our actions feeling like more like a "have to" or "should".

Remember, it is not what we are doing that creates. It is our state of being while we are doing it. So inspired action could be taking out the trash, or going for a walk on the beach or calling that person that just popped into your mind. It doesn't have to be some huge sweeping life altering action. In fact, it typically is not, although it could be. Please, just don't "wait" for it.

Now this will scare some of you. Sometimes you shouldn't take any physical action. *What?!?* I know, but here is the thing. If you take action from a state of fear, your action is a waste of your time and energy because it will never be in alignment with what you want. It will just manifest more fear.

One of my clients was frustrated because two clients owed her money. She had been chasing them for a while to make payments, but to no avail.

She decided she wanted them to pay and she

stopped trying to get them to do anything. Then she stayed in alignment with her desire by being aware and accepting her state of being. Within one week she was paid—not by one, but by both!

When you start to trust your intuition you will notice that sometimes things just "fall into your lap," which of course they never really do. You've just unconsciously created them.

Maybe you'll take an action, but it won't be a direct action. For example I read a great book, *The Magician's Way* by William Whitecloud, and had the thought that I should contact him and ask if he would be willing to be interviewed by me. Instead of contacting him right away, I sent an email out to my newsletter list recommending his book.

About a week later he contacted me! He said that he noticed that I had sent a bunch of folks his way who bought his book. Not only did he do the interview, since then we have worked together and I even wrote a book recommendation for his second book, *The Last Shaman*.

So, how can you remain open to inspired action? Be *willing* to know what action you want to take next and then don't second-guess it when it comes in.

Since you have made a commitment to be aware, then you will automatically be open to hearing intuition. The tough part will be you being willing not to talk yourself out of it.

You have a thought, "I should call Jack." If you are committed to taking inspired action you would pick up the phone and call Jack. But what might you typically do? Have a conversation in your head along the lines of, "I haven't talked to Jack in years. I'm not even sure I know what I would say to him. He would think I was crazy if I called him out of the blue. I'm not going to call Jack, it just doesn't make any sense."

The good news is you now have the great "tool" of acceptance to help ensure that you follow through on your inspired action. How do use acceptance to ensure you follow through? Let's go back to calling Jack...

I should call Jack. I haven't talked to Jack in years. I accept that I'm experiencing fear right now, that's okay... *I'm not even sure I know what I would say to him.* I accept that I'm experiencing confusion right now, and that's okay...*He would think I was crazy if I called him out of the blue.* I accept that I'm experiencing judgment right now, that's okay....*I'm not going to call Jack, it just doesn't make any sense.* I accept I'm experiencing resistance right now, that's okay...*What the hell, I'll give it a shot.* I accept I'm experiencing possibility right now, that's okay...

Here is a good benchmark to knowing when your intuition is speaking up, the more it *doesn't* make sense, the more you are guaranteed that it is your intuition.

Our conscious mind needs to be able to rationalize what we think, say, or do. It needs to rationalize because it doesn't have all the information. Infinite Mind/Universe sees everything and therefore doesn't need to rationalize anything because it knows everything.

Intuition comes in many packages. This is one of my favorite examples. I was in Starbucks one day with my daughter. I noticed a "regular" sitting next to me. He was pouring over dog racing sheets, which I had seen him do many times before. Sammi and I were playing and I called her a "Chatty Cathy." She asked what that was and I told her. We had a good laugh and left.

Several days later, I was in Starbucks again. I was sitting with a friend when the gentleman, the same "regular" with the racing sheets, next to us asked, "Were you the one who was in here a couple of days ago talking about being a "Chatty Cathy?"

I said yes and he said this is the most amazing thing. He said that he was looking at a racing sheet and at the exact moment I said, "Chatty Cathy," he read the name of a dog, "Chatty Cathy." He thought that was interesting, but didn't bet on the dog. You guessed it: Chatty Cathy won and paid out 18 to 1. He said it was like God was talking directly to him and he didn't listen!

So what should you do? *Call Jack!* How many times in your life have you thought of someone and they called you? Or you did take a chance and make that phone call that made no sense and the person on the other end was thinking about you? This is the magic that happens when we stop relying solely on our conscious mind and open up to the infinite mind that is running everything in our lives according to the states of being we are choosing.

Think of it like this: Your life is one puzzle piece of a huge puzzle. Your conscious mind can only see what is on your piece. Infinite mind sees the whole puzzle and therefore knows how all the pieces fit together. When we ignore our intuition we are basically slowing down the fruition of what we desire. The fastest path to all that you want to experience is to keep your attention on what you want and take the inspired action that comes to you, as it comes to you.

Sometimes we won't listen to our intuition. My friend was in the grocery store the other day and she had the thought, "I should get some chocolate chips." Then she thought, "I don't really need them," so she didn't get them. That night her daughter wanted to make chocolate chip cookies but couldn't because there weren't any chocolate chips!

And sometimes we *will* listen. I had the thought recently to suggest to one of my business clients that I coach his staff as well to help him meet his business objectives. I don't normally have these types of thoughts—a good sign that intuition had kicked in—so I followed it.

I sent him an email and he said he would check in with his staff to see what they thought. I found out later that before I sent the email, his staff had already had a discussion about how they would like to work with me because they could see how my client, their boss, had changed. It would be interesting if I could figure out the timing of this, when their discussion was and when I had the thought. I'd bet they were pretty close in time.

Wouldn't you rather listen and therefore get closer and closer to what you desire than to not listen and get further and further away?

So to be a conscious creator instead of being an unconscious creator you have to be willing to:

1.   Be aware and accept your state of being.

2.   Get clear on what you want.

3.   Identify the states of being you will experience when you experience the *result* you want and be willing to experience them *now*. When you aren't, you simply accept whatever state of being you are experiencing.

4.   Get quiet and claim, "I AM."

5.   Experience the states of being by claiming, "I AM [fill in the blank]," the states of being that will create your end result.

6.   Pop your simple, visceral visual.

7.   Be aware and accept your state of being!

Now what do you do when you apply the 7 steps of conscious creation and nothing seems to be happening?

—Chapter 5

Conscious Creation Trouble Shooting

Here are some common challenges—and their solutions—that people often face when implementing conscious creation in their life.

Questioning your role as a conscious creator and the role of the Universe to deliver the "how."

Think of the Universe like your GPS. When using your GPS you need a destination. You have to be clear on your end result. Once you put in the final destination the GPS gives you exact, step-by-step instructions on how to get there. These are steps you could never plan because you've never taken them before. You don't know they exist yet.

Not only are you given step-by-step instructions, you are also given the best instruction at that moment because your GPS takes into account traffic and construction. It takes into account more than you ever could because it sees the whole picture while you only see bits and pieces. So your job is to know exactly where you want to go and then follow the directions given; the GPS does the rest.

Now think of how you consciously create. When you know exactly what you want you are basically entering your desire into the Universe. The Universe then creates the exact path to your desire. Like GPS the Universe sees the best path because it sees everything! So like in the case of GPS your job is to know exactly what you want and then follow the step-by-step directions given and the Universe does the rest.

Simple right? But what do we do instead?

- We give vague destinations because we are unclear. We can put "gas station" into our GPS and we'll get a whole bunch of locations, but not necessarily the one we need. When we aren't clear with the Universe we get results, but usually not results that we really want because the Universe can't give us what we don't know we want.

- We don't trust. How many times have we questioned our GPS. It says go right, we say that can't be right and we go left. We end up going out of our way or getting to our destination, but only after we get redirected by our GPS. Same with the Universe, we think we know better, but we forget that we don't see the whole picture and while it might "make sense" to go left, the Universe knows that going right is going to be the fastest way.

- We change our mind. What happens when

you put a destination in a GPS? You are guaranteed to get there. What happens when you change your destination? You are guaranteed to get to the new destination, but if you change the directions four steps in, you can't get to your destination anymore.

If all you do is keep changing your final destination, then you'll never get anywhere. What do you think happens with the Universe? The same exact thing! If you keep changing your desires, you keep changing your destination. You can't blame the Universe—like GPS it will continue to give you the exact directions to any desire you want, but it can't make you stick with it.

▪ We think we know better. The other day I put in my final destination in my GPS. Since I had been there before, I kind-of knew where I was going so when the directions popped up I was surprised it wasn't anywhere near what I thought. I decided that maybe I didn't know better and I followed the directions. I got there and when I reversed the destination to get home, I got the directions I was expecting originally. Turns out there had been an accident on the highway that I'd thought I should take and that's why the directions were different than what I thought. I'm glad I decided that maybe I didn't know better. I realized that I often don't think the Universe knows better. Remember intuition can seem nonsensical. I may be on the way to the desire I want, but will often do what I think will work instead of following the instruction of the Universe.

So what should we do to leverage the power of the Universe?

- Enter clear desires. Be clear on what you want. Know that whatever you want is a desire that can be filled and deserves to be filled.
- Trust the steps that come up and take them. Unfortunately, the Universe does not spit out numbered steps like your GPS. Its steps come in the form of intuition. So stay clear on your destination and do anything that comes from an inspired place.
- Stay steadfast in your desire until you get there. Stop changing your desire when you think things aren't happening. The Universe is always working and you have no way of knowing what it is doing so just stay focused on what you want and take the inspired action you are being given.

Settling

How can you ever experience what you want if

you consistently settle for less than what you want? It's impossible. Settling is the action manifested from a state of being of doubt and limitation.

When you see something that is kind-of what you want, but not really, just accept that you are experiencing doubt and be willing to consider that you could have exactly what you want. This is the only way to ensure that you get exactly what you want.

As one client writes, *"Remember last summer I wanted the BMW convertible? I found several but never acted on the purchase... because they weren't 100% what I wanted. Well, last week—I saw one parked in the lot where I work—and I just happened to see the owner getting into it. I pulled up and started chatting with him—and after about a 30 minute convo found out he was thinking of selling. I'm going for an inspection with a mechanic next week and barring anything major, I'm ready to buy!! This one is more in line with what I want price-wise and the color is what I want... the others were not really the right thing."*

You fall off the awareness, acceptance, attention wagon.

In my own experience, and my experience with clients, I've noticed that there are two reasons why it is easy to stop being aware, accepting our state of being, and keeping our attention on what we want.

The first is not so obvious—when things start going well. That's right, when things start going better people start slacking off. They forget what got them the results in the first place. The best way to stay ahead of this is to be sure that you are taking "creative credit" for your results.

As you consciously create you will notice internal and external results. Internal results always precede external results.

Internal results could be a new thought you've had about a situation, or you notice that you didn't react like you typically have in the past to a situation. It could also be that you are experiencing new ideas, having new inspirations, and taking new actions.

You will know them because they will be different than what you've experienced in the past. You will also be feeling more acceptance states of being so you will notice that you are experiencing more possibility, happiness, peace, and calm.

"It is amazing how much more I am getting done effortlessly now that I am accepting. I have found that when I am accepting my state of being I am not identifying with my thoughts or feelings. This creates a lot of space for me to focus on my wants instead of trying to justify why I am having unpleasant thoughts and feelings.

Exhilarating is what it is like to see my internal

results. I have more patience, I laugh more, and have just been generally happier. The more I pay attention internally the easier it becomes to identify my state of being and move forward if needed.

On the tennis court this week I miss-hit a very simple shot. In my head I was calling myself every four-letter word. Then I accepted and turned my focus to the feeling I get when I hit a winner. (Such a great feeling!) I was able to move past the negativity and flow into my happy place quickly, by accepting my state of being. I may have lost the match but I was at peace throughout the game."

Early on in my own experience with acceptance I had been scheduled to do a speech for an organization. Presentation time finally arrived, but without my knowledge, it actually arrived a day earlier!

I had it in my head that I was scheduled for Sunday, so imagine my surprise when I got a call Saturday morning from the coordinator asking me where I was. Where was I? In Massachusetts in my pajamas, giving my daughter a bath. Where I was *supposed to be* was in Connecticut, on the stage within the next half-hour. Imagine my horror! Of course all I could do was apologize, and so I did, but the *real* work started after I hung up the phone.

All the judgments kicked in. "How could you be so stupid? You don't deserve opportunities like that!

Why are you doing this work, you can't even get it right!" and on and on. But I was willing to accept, not the thoughts and judgments, but my state of being—shame, guilt, fear. I just stayed with them and accepted and as I did, *I was free.* I did not beat myself up and I knew that it all unfolding perfectly!

You see the *fact* was that I missed my presentation. As soon I missed it, it was in the past and didn't exist anymore. The *story*, which is never true, was that I was a terrible businessperson because I missed my presentation. The only true *experience* in that moment was my state of being and accepting it every step of the way freed me! It allowed me to move through the not-so-comfortable states and back into the state of peace.

What effect did my accepting have on this business relationship? Seven years later I am still doing coaching and presentations for them!

External results are more obvious. You are creating the experiences you want or you are creating even beyond your expectations.

Bottom line, you want to consciously take credit for all your results, internal and external. Why? Because then you are tying them back to the fact that you are the one creating them. When you take creative credit you are reminding yourself that *you* did it and as you take ownership you will be less likely to lose awareness.

My client had been very diligent in accepting her

state of being no matter what it was. She was looking to find an alternative to a lease she was locked into, either finding a way to share the space, or getting out of the lease completely. She was willing to know that the right opportunity would present itself and she accepted her state of being of doubt when she was resisting that that she what she wanted.

Then she got an offer, but it wasn't what she really wanted. So she was willing to know that the perfect deal was still on its way. Then she said, "Out of the blue, the perfect deal came in!"

What state of being are you in when you say "out of the blue"? Believe it or not, the state of limitation. What you are saying is that you believe that you have no power over what comes into your experience, it's just dumb luck. Nothing is ever "out of the blue" because you are always creating, either consciously or unconsciously. Own it!

The second reason we stop being aware, accepting our state of being, and keeping our attention on what we want is more obvious—when things don't seem to be happening or they aren't happening fast enough. This is a critical point in your application, and therefore in your ability to get the results you want. When you think nothing is happening, that's when you want to hammer away at acceptance, and I mean hammer!

Has anything ever been achieved if someone has quit? Nope. So how can you expect to get results if you give up on the process that will get you the results? You can't!

And this is the icing on the cake, according to all you've learned. If you are experiencing frustration, disappointment, and impatience, and you aren't aware, you are only going to create more opportunities to experience frustration, disappointment, and impatience!

The fastest way to get back on track is to accept that you are experiencing frustration and that's okay. Then commit to being aware and accepting as much as possible and I mean as *much* as possible. Then you will naturally become interested and newly invigorated in regards to your end result. Some of my clients have said that it was when they became an "acceptance machine" that they were able to get past the disappointment and frustration and get what they wanted.

One of my clients had a business partner who wasn't making agreed upon payments. This of course caused my client to not be able to make the payments *he* needed to make. He spent months experiencing disappointment and therefore getting caught up in how it was impossible for him to get the money owed him through this partner.

He called me because he knew in his heart that his state of being and subsequent thoughts were not in alignment with the end result he wanted which was a strong partnership where he was paid all that was owed and all future payments were paid consistently and on time.

He was experiencing disappointment but was willing to become an "acceptance machine" to create a change.

It wasn't easy, and one weekend he hit the wall and was about to give up. He kept worrying and was stuck in the "how" which was a perspective that said that they couldn't possibly pay him by the time he needed them to. He started thinking that he should send them a letter that demanded payment, but he knew that he was in resistance and together we kept him on track with acceptance.

After hammering away on acceptance throughout the weekend he started knowing that everything would work out.

The next week he had a meeting, unrelated to this issue, at his partner's company. While he was there he had the thought to see if someone he knew at the company would be available to chat, not about the money issue, just to say hello.

The person was available and so they met. During the conversation the person asked how the partnership was going. My client was honest, and just let him know the status. The person immediately called the director of finance and had him come down to talk with my client.

They were introduced and the finance director asked if my client happened to know so-and-so. Turns out that so-and-so was my client's sister-in-law, who was instrumental in helping the finance director's mother with a health issue. He was so grateful to my client and his sister-in-law that he immediately jumped on the payment issue and now my client has been paid all that was owed him and all additional payments are being made in full on time!

Do you think any of this could have happened if my client continued to experience disappointment, frustration, and impatience and chose not to hammer away at acceptance? You just have to look at the results he was getting before he recommitted to acceptance. NONE!

When you hammer away at acceptance you will naturally start to, what I like to call, "allow the delays," which keep you on track to all that you want.

"Each fall I take my boat out of covered moorage on the water and put it on a trailer and store it in a commercial rental storage place on land.

Last week I contacted the company I had been with last year. They said they did not have anything available as people just aren't traveling in their RVs so much, so nothing is opening up. But, because I am a repeat customer they would put me on the top of a waiting list for covered storage. I needed the storage finalized by this week.

Well, I accepted that I was experiencing concern. I accepted I was experiencing loss, I was experiencing frustration, I was experiencing resistance, I was experiencing limitation, and that was all okay.

Saturday night I got a message that an opening had come available but it was larger than I needed so the price was $190 per month. I had paid $150 per month last year. They gave me until the next afternoon to decide. I accepted that I was experiencing resistance, lack, need, pressure, and it was all okay.

So, it came down to two hours before I committed to them. I accepted that I was experiencing limitation, resistance, lack, and frustration, and it was okay. Instead of giving into the negative situation that I was experiencing I sat down at the computer and started to search for alternatives. Believe me it is not easy to find covered storage areas for boats on trailers where I live. I looked online and made a few calls to no avail. I accepted that I was experiencing lack and it was okay, over and over.

I made one last call, to be my final call, and the director told me they did not have covered storage for boats but one of their other facilities did and she thought there was one unexpected opening that just came up.

She gave me their number and I called them. The director there said that, yes, they just got an opening and it was the only one they had and I could have it if I wanted it.

I accepted that I was experiencing abundance and happiness and success and luck and good fortune, and it was all okay.

The bonus was the cost is only $105 per month. I drove by there today and it is a perfect spot.

I never would have imagined this storage location even existed. It is closer to my home and more convenient than previous storage locations I have used.

I accept that I am experiencing abundance and it is okay!"

My client applied acceptance and was therefore able to "allow the delay" which led him to an even better result than he expected. That's what happens when you learn how to apply acceptance and then use it to consciously create what you want.

So use frustration and disappointment as "green" flags to remind you that it is time for you to be very aware and willing to hammer away at acceptance.

What will your consistency and perseverance when dealing with these challenges lead to? I don't know what it will lead to for you. That's completely up to you. I do know it has lead to some amazing results for my clients.

Internal Results...

"I am more focused."

"I am less worried."

"I have better health."

"I am more confident."

"Harmony."

"I stopped beating myself up."

"I trust myself now."

"I experience less need."

"I am now honest with myself and others."

"I finally stopped comparing myself with others."

"I'm clear on what I want, not what I think I should want."

"All my relationships are better."

"Insights."

"Peace."

"I am more open to happiness and goodness."

"I've had powerful insights about my relationship with myself."

"I have more peace with those around me."

"I am no longer a victim of my emotions."

"I feel real freedom."

"I have much better emotional health."

"I have been released from overwhelm, sadness, and fear."

"I am finally open to a new relationship."

"I have a lot more hope."

"I take much more action in the direction I really want."

External Results...

"When we started, one of my goals was to create 100K within 60 days. I have closed almost 60K in deals over the last three weeks! 40K or more to go!"

"As promised I'm emailing to let you know that I have been successful in receiving a job offer. All thanks to the techniques you taught me. The offer came through yesterday, which was five days later than the end-of-January time I had been visualizing myself to be in work. However, I am thrilled with the offer as it was with the company I really wanted to work for, it's a newly created position giving me a free hand to make the job my own, and it is for a salary considerably higher than I'd anticipated. Although it is not much closer to home than my previous job, their building lease is expiring later this year and one of my responsibilities is to find another building for them. So you can guess where I'll be looking first."

"I was experiencing scarcity and worry about money. I accepted it. We have tickets to see Billy Joel at the New Orleans Jazz Fest. I started thinking we shouldn't

go because of money. Too far to drive, etc. And I still have to pay the phone, electric, and cable bill this month. I accepted my state of being.

I was up all night and couldn't sleep. I was miserable the next day and I'm driving to my gig. I am accepting for an hour in the car that I am experiencing crankiness, sleep deprivation, yucky, and blah. I didn't even want to play my sax.

We get there to the gig, start setting up, and the manager of the venue comes over and asks me if I am booked for New Year's Eve.

I said 'no' cause it's still eight months away and I never book NYE this far in advance!! Long story short he books me on the spot! I should be getting a deposit in two weeks or so!!!"

"Since our last call my relationship with my son Alex has changed like from night to day. I've been able to give him the love he needs without feeling overwhelmed. On the contrary it has been a joy, and he has started being able to spend more time away from me. THANK YOU SOOOO MUCH!!!! You don't know the gift you just gave me by helping me love my son with an open heart."

"I took your advice. As I've been washing my face, looking in the mirror, putting on make-up—doing all the

things that usually bring on the awareness of my skin issues—I've tried saying to myself that I understand that I'm currently in a state of being of frustration and worry over my skin and that it's okay. It helps me feel lighter in the moment and also helps me not to dwell on the issue for more than a few seconds.

My skin has made a huge improvement! It looks about 80% better and feels better too, more normal and balanced. It's almost not even an issue anymore and was one of the biggest things that I worried about just a few weeks ago. Anyway, I'm going to keep practicing this and I wanted to thank you again for giving me the tools and insight I needed in order to really use the law of attraction in a positive and effective way in my life. Thanks so much!"

"It's amazing how things change when you start accepting your state of being!

Remember the condo I was trying to sell that we'd been talking about? I had been accepting I'm experiencing fear and doubt all day yesterday after our call and early this morning, a buyer called me about it and now we're writing an offer for her. If both buyer and seller agree to the terms, then we are even going to double-end the deal.

The seller also told my business partner that we need to meet one day so we can talk about where they will purchase.

I'm finally getting this! Thank you for all your help!"

"I feel so 'unstuck' right now that it's amazing! I am so busy creating the perfect relationship for me right now that potential guys seem to be jumping out of the woodwork!"

"Um!!! WOW!!!! My husband just walked in here with twenty one-hundred-dollar bills!!! Some unexpected business and they paid cash upfront!!!!!!!!!!! I AM A POWERFUL CREATOR!"

"OK, here is acceptance at its best. I have been short of money so I have been accepting need and was realizing that I don't need money to experience freedom and relief etc., that those states of being are available to me right now. So, yesterday I receive a call and got an unexpected $1500. Today I receive an email for another $850.

Then the REAL spooky thing...Someone mentioned the name of a company to me yesterday and I wrote the name down figuring I could contact them for potential business. I never heard of them so this morning I went online and wrote down their name and number and was about to call them to find out who their president was so

I could introduce myself for opportunities to work together.

As I was literally picking up the phone to dial, I received an email from another client of mine who had already introduced me to the president, via email, of the exact same company I was going to contact! They have a need for a recruiter for a project right now!

I was floored as the theme from the Twilight Zone was playing in my mind. Wow."

When you are willing to consciously use your creative power to create what **you** want, you end up helping others get what they want. This, my friend, is your greatest gift.

- Mike took his love of kids and sports and created a company that helps young athletes not only perform better on the field, but more importantly in their lives. http://nolimitsmentaledge.com

- Kerry took her love of helping people and raw food and created a business where she runs Green Smoothie Cleanse Seminars. http://www.queenofgreens.com.au

- Greg Kuhn took his love of writing and

now thousands of people are getting the help they need understanding quantum physics and how they can leverage it to create the lives they want.

http://whyquantumphysicists.com

The list goes on and on...

What do you love? Do you understand that the longer you wait to honor that love the more you're not only depriving yourself, but others of what they want and love?

Now that you know what your power is and how to tap into it consciously you really have no more excuses. If you think you do, then just accept that you are experiencing limitation and be willing to consider that creating what you love could be fun and exciting. Then it will be!

—Epilogue

According to an old Hindu legend, "There was once a time when all human beings were gods, but they so abused their divinity that Brahma, the chief god, decided to take it away from them and hide it where it could never be found.

Where to hide their divinity was the question. So Brahma called a council of the gods to help him decide. 'Let's bury it deep in the earth,' said the gods. But Brahma answered, 'No, that will not do because humans will dig into the earth and find it.' Then the gods said, 'Let's sink it in the deepest ocean.' But Brahma said, 'No, not there, for they will learn to dive into the ocean and will find it.' Then the gods said, 'Let's take it to the top of the highest mountain and hide it there.' But once again Brahma replied, 'No, that will not do either, because they will eventually climb every mountain and once again take up their divinity.' Then the gods gave up and said, 'We do not know where to hide it, because it seems that there is no place on earth or in the sea that human beings will not eventually reach.'

Brahma thought for a long time and then said, 'Here is what we will do. We will hide their divinity deep in the center of their own being, for humans will never think to look for it there.'

All the gods agreed that this was the perfect hiding place, and the deed was done. And since that time humans have been going up and down the earth, digging, diving, climbing, and exploring—searching for something already within themselves."

~ Author Unknown

ABOUT THE AUTHORS

Doreen Banaszak

Since leaving behind corporate America over a decade ago, Doreen Banaszak has been helping thousands of people through her books, seminars, and coaching to create the changes they desire in their lives. She does this by teaching her clients how to turn their attention inward and harness the power that has always been within them. Her books include *Excuse Me, Your Life Is Now; Excuse Me, College Is Now;* and *The Power of Acceptance.*

www.doreenbanaszak.com

Arden Rembert Brink

With a varied background ranging from business executive, non-profit director, house designer, and small business consultant, throughout it all Arden Rembert Brink has written, whether the end product be media plans, fund raising proposals, ad copy, websites and brochures, or articles for the trade. Upon moving to Costa Rica in 2006, she decided to turn her writing attention to books and blogs, which she continued upon her return to the states in 2012. Her books include *Unraveling the Mysteries of Moving to Costa Rica* and *Reality Check, A Real-Life Look at Living in Paradise* (Release date, July 2015), and *The Power of Acceptance.* She lives in Utah with her husband, assorted 4-legged creatures, and along with being a writer is a happy caregiver for her grandchildren.

ardenrembertbrink.com